UNSOLICITED COMMENTS ABOUT THIS REVELATION MESSAGE:

The Messianic Revelation Series offers an entirely different perspective on Revelation than any books on Revelation you may have read before. The reason is simple. *The Messianic Revelation Series* takes into account the Hebraic background and mindset of the Jewish writer of Revelation. This approach brings startling new clarity to the prophetic message of Revelation for our day. Following are unsolicited comments about this message left by Tsiyon Radio listeners at the www.tsiyon.org web site:

"Teaching from a Hebraic perspective/understanding gives the Book of Revelation a new "life.""

"This was a really good teaching. So much that has been missing from the traditional message."

"This grand vision sheds new light on some very "old" things."

"The strength of Brother Eliyahu's teachings for me is in his ability to show us things that we've seen many times before in an entirely new and compelling way."

"Very good, I like how U gave the foundational background about Revelations and about the writer too."

"There is much to be learned here and perhaps a few challenges to old beliefs to be faced, but overall, this is a "walk" worth taking."

"It gave a better understanding of what the book of Revelation is all about, a better view of it, & I want to hear more."

"Wow, that was very good. I hardly had room to put all my notes."

"Thank you Eliyahu. Can't wait for the rest of the series. Shalom."

"Once again, very clear historical facts presented by Eliyahu, and tied into every area of past, present and future events."

"The positives far outweigh the negatives in the reality of Y'shua's judgments."

"I liked the description about the throne room."

"I am amazed that Eliyahu got to see into the throne room."

“Shalom Eliyahu! Thank you for yet another exciting connection of YHWH’s divine purpose in the world economic crisis.”

“This message gave me a completely different perspective on what it means to be an “overcomer.””

“That was very good, excellent. I can’t wait to hear more about the white horse.”

“Don’t waste another day - we’re running out of time!”

“This message is a shake-up/wake-up call to all of those who profess belief in our Messiah Y’shua.”

“We look with anticipation to YHWH for righteous judgment, as HE alone is worthy to be Judge, having the perfect solution, dealing with the rebellion that has turned HIS creation up-side down!”

“I found myself walking alongside Yochanan into the Throne room of Heaven.”

“This message will challenge many to consider the Four Horsemen of Revelation in a new way.”

“I love the emphasis on having right relationship with YAHWEH, Who alone can and will protect those who are righteous.”

“This message “paints” being an overcomer in a much more positive and encouraging light.”

“I encourage those that have a heart to be “overcomers” to come and hear and then to “be doers of the WORD.”

“Compromise for the sake of unity, mixture for the sake of compromise and conformity for the so-called “good” don’t fit HIS definition of the “narrow path.””

“[This] Revelation message has given me new information to consider, points of contention to meditate on and broken down barriers to new ways of looking at things.”

“Patience is key to receiving the fullness of all that HE is bringing here to HIS people. Stay the course and reap the benefits of walking this out with HIM.”

The Messianic Revelation Series
Volume 1

Annoucing:
Judgment Day

Eliyahu ben David

Zarach

Author Online!

For radio programs, audio CDs, news, and more visit Eliyahu ben David at:

www.Tsiyon.org

www.RevelationSeries.com

Published by
Zarach
Salt Lake City, Utah

ISBN-10: 0967947154
ISBN-13: 9780967947150

Subject heading:
REL101000 RELIGION / Messianic Judaism
REL006140 RELIGION / Biblical Studies / Prophecy
REL006070 RELIGION / Biblical Commentary / New Testament

Except as otherwise noted, Scripture passages herein are quoted from the Hebrew Names Version of the World English Bible (HNV). See Conventions and Bibliography for more information on Scripture usage.

Cover art and book Illustrations by Eliyahu ben David

1.0

Contents

UNSOLICITED COMMENTS ABOUT THIS REVELATION MESSAGE: 1

1. MESSIANIC REVELATION

WHY THE TSIYON INTERPRETATION OF REVELATION IS SO DIFFERENT! 15

The Book Of Revelation Reveals Our Future 16

A Unique Perspective On Revelation 16

Digging In To Revelation 18

The Purpose Of Revelation 19

Is "The Lord's Day" Sunday? 20

Yochanan–an Exhaustive Witness 21

Establishing The Writer Of Revelation 22

Receive The Blessing Of Revelation! 23

From Whom, To Whom, Hebraic Greeting 23

Y'shua The Messiah, The Faithful Witness 24

A Torah Covenant Promise Fulfilled 25

The Coming Of The Messiah Of The Hebrew Prophets 25

The God Of Israel 26

Yochanan, Your Brother In Tribulation 26

The Heart Of Yochanan Revealed 27

When Revelation Was Written And Why That Matters 29

The Revelation Is "Thoroughly Jewish" 30

A Hebraic View Of Revelation 31

Revelation–A Jewish Apocalypse 32

Jewish Apocalyptic Genre Is Predictive Of The Future! 32

Why Every Interpretation You Have Ever Heard Of Revelation Is Wrong 33

The Tsiyon Exegetic Approach 34

2. MESSIAH JUDGES HIS OWN

MESSIAH REVEALED AS PRIEST-JUDGE 37

Messiah Comes As High Priest 37

Messiah As Priest-Judge Judges His Own 38

The Seven Menorahs 38
The Seven Menorahs Are The Seven Assemblies 39
The Seven Stars 40
Judgment Must Always Come To God's Own First 40
Judgment On The House Of God In The NT 41
Judgment May Be For Or Against 41
A Dual Fulfillment Of This Revelation Prophecy 42
Structure Of The Judgments Of The Seven Assemblies 43
Judgments Of Commendation In The Assemblies 44
Do Commendations Of Messiah Reflect Your Behavior? 45
Judgments Of Sin In The Assemblies 46
Messiah Judges Sins Of Believers 46
Judgment Of Rewards To "Him Who Overcomes" 47
Be An Overcomer! 48
What Is An Overcomer? 48
How Overcomers Receive The Rewards 49
Parable Of The Overcomers 49
Grasp The Prize! 50
Judgments Of Punishment Against Believers 50
Unrepentant Sinners Are Punished! 51
Judgments Of Punishment Against Assemblies 52
Un-repented Sin Brings Punishment To The Assemblies 52
What Became Of The Seven Assemblies? 52

3. MESSIAH JUDGES HIS OWN-AGAIN
LAST DAYS JUDGMENT OF THE HOUSE OF GOD 57
Sins Of The Church System Judged By Messiah 57
God Doesn't Judge With Favoritism 58
Raptured Or Removed? 58
All Who Profess Belief In Messiah Included 59
Judgment Made Manifest 59
Examine The Evidence Of Messiah's Judgment 60
4,392 Accusations Of Abuse Engulf Catholic Clergy 60
2008—Pope States He Is Shamed By Sexual Ause Scandals 61

1,676 Reports Of Abuse By Denominational Leaders 61
High Profile Evangelical Scandals 61
List Of Christian Evangelists Involved in High Profile Scandals 62
Scandal Overturns Leader Of 30,000,000 USA Evangelicals 62
Let's Summarize The Evidence 63
The News Reports Furnish The Evidence 64
Judgment Focused On Leaders Of The Church System 65
Why You Have Never Heard This Before 65
An Attack Of The Enemy? 66
Please Don't Kill The Messenger! 66
Evidence That Demands A Verdict 67
Judgment Has Started With The House Of God 67
40 Years Of Judgment 68
Israel's 40 Years Of Judgment In The Wilderness 68
Judgment Allows Time For Correction And Repentance 69
The Judgment Of YHWH Is Good! 69
Overcomers Seized The Promise! 70
Israel Immersed Into Messiah At The Red Sea 70
The Tragic Outcome For The Wilderness Generation 71
Cheap Grace Doesn't Cut It! 72
40 Years Wilderness Judgment-Our Example 72
Paul's Message Doesn't Sound "Christian" 72
A Message For The Ends Of The Ages 73
The End Of The Age Started In 1967 73
Paul's Three 40-Year Parallel Judgment Periods 74
The 40-Year Judgment Period Of The Church System 74
Where Is The Punishment? 75
Now The Tribulation Will Start, Right?..Not! 75
Adopt The Overcomer Mindset! 76

4. VISITING HEAVEN'S COURTROOM
THE JUDGMENT COURT REVEALED 79
What Are We Looking At? 79
The Calendar 80

The Throne Was Set 80
The Porch Of Judgment 81
One Sat On The Throne 83
A Rainbow Around The Throne Like Emerald 83
Around The Throne Were 24 Thrones 84
On The Thrones Were 24 Elders Sitting 86
Elders Of The Tribes Of Israel 86
Elders Of The Kingdom Of Israel 87
The 24 Elders 88
Lightnings And Thunders And Sounds 89
YHWH Bound Himself To The Mosaic Covenant 90
Why The World Hates Israel 91
Why The World Is In The Wrong 91
Before His Throne 92
Why Simple Translation Errors Occur 93
In The Gaze Of The Throne 93
Seven Lamps Of Fire 94
Seven Spirits Of God In Zechariah 94
Seven Eyes Or Seven Lamps? 94
Standing On The Sea Of Glass 95
Similar To Crystal 96
The Big Picture 97

5. JUDGMENT DAY
COURT IS NOW IN SESSION! 99
Four Live Things 100
Live Things In Ezekiel 101
Why These Four Are Called: ***Alive!*** 101
Full Of Eyes 101
Four Angels Of The Presence 102
A Lion, A Young Bull, A Man, And A Flying Eagle? 102
Six Wings 103
Full Of Eyes–Again 104
About The Book Of Enoch 104

Enoch Saw It First 105
For The Elect...In The Day Of Tribulation 106
Enoch's Old, Sad Story Of Rebellion 107
Men Implore The Four To Make Their Suit 107
Temporary Measures–Then Docketed For Judgment Day 108
The Declaration 109
Perspective On The Declaration Of The Four Live Things 109
An Open And Shut Case 110
The Indictment Of The Rebels Established 110
A Damnable Crime 111
Is This You? 111
24 Elders Cast Their Crowns 112
The Moral Imperative In The Cry Of The Righteous 112
Rebels Deny YHWH His Due 113
The Walk Of The Righteous Convicts The Wicked 113
Summary Of The Case Now Before The Judgment Court 114
Charges Against The Rebellion Include: 114
Other Facts Requiring Closure 115
Response Of The King 115
We Don't Have To Guess 116
His Royal Decree 116
Not A Book–A Scroll 117
Within And Behind 117
A Perfect Solution In Hand! 118
Sealed With Seven Seals 118
Not Like The Pictures 119
A Progressive Judgment On An Appointed Schedule 119
Hurry Up–And Wait 120

6. THE LION OF JUDAH STANDS UP
THE LAMB'S DAY OF POWER 123
A Call Goes Forth 123
Weeping In Heaven 124
Our Jewish Champion In Heaven 124

Lion Of The Tribe Of Judah Foretold 125
The Puzzle Rapidly Fills In 125
Eleven More Last Days Prophecies 126
The Destiny of Israel 126
Root Of David 127
The Lion Is A Lamb 127
Passover Lamb 128
Cut Off For The Disobedience Of My People, Israel 128
Only A Lion Could Be This Lamb 129
Focus On Israel 129
Sit And Wait 130
Stand, And Stop Waiting! 130
The Lamb's Day Of Power 131
Symbols Of The Lamb's Power 132
None Like Him! 132
Prophetic Shorthand Weaves In Zechariah 133
Four Horns And Four Winds In Zechariah 133
4 Horns=4 Beasts Of Daniel=Gentile Nations 134
Seven Trumps Four–Israel Re-Gathered 134
Seven Eyes In Zechariah 135
Seven Eyes See The Temple Of Zerubbabel Completed 135
A Type Of The Spiritual Temple 136
What Is The Spiritual Temple? 136
Uniquely Qualified To Get The Job Done 137
What The Man Reveals About The Mission 137
Early Indications Of The Contents Of The Scroll 138
He Took The Scroll! 138
Two Versions Of What Happened Next 138
The Live Things And The 24 Elders Worship The Lamb 139
A New Song 140
Covenant Promise To Obedient Israel 141
A Remnant As "My Own Possession" 141
A Covenant Kingdom And Priests 142
Our Blessed Hope 142

Worthy Is The Lamb! 143
The Lamb Will Get The Job Done! 143

7. SEALS HAVE BEEN OPENED
MYSTERY OF THE FOUR HORSEMEN REVEALED 145
Opening Of The First Seal 145
Opening Of The Second Seal 146
Opening Of The Third Seal 147
Opening Of The Fourth Seal 147
Origin Of Four Horsemen Apocalyptic Motif 147
Zechariah Prophesied For And To Remnant Of Israel 148
Four Horsemen Of Zechariah 150
The Report Of The Horsemen To The Angel 151
The Response Of YHWH To The Report Of The Horsemen 151
The Four Horsemen Of Zechariah Ride For Israel 152
Four Charioteers Of Zechariah Ride The Four Winds 152
Three Separate Missions 153
Riders Of The Four Winds 153
Four Archangels Send Four Riders Into Four Winds 154
Unlocking The Mystery Of The 4 Riders Of Revelation 154
Significance Of Varied Missions 155
The First Seal Revealed 156
The Second Seal Revealed 158
Checking The Compass In Heaven 159
The Third Seal Revealed 160
The Fourth Seal Revealed 161
It's About Israel—And You 163
What We Can Expect From The Four Horsemen 165
The Ending Point—The Starting Point 166

EPILOGUE 167
Suejean's Observations 170
Dawn's Observations 172
The Author's Final Remarks 176

ILLUSTRATIONS
Seven Assemblies Of Revelation 36
Heavenly Judgment Court 78
Release Of The Four Horsemen 144

CONVENTIONS AND BIBLIOGRAPHY 181
Scripture Usage and Conventions Herein 181
Strong's Number Usage and Conventions Herein 183
Bible Software References Used 184
Print Books Cited or Consulted Herein 184
Ten Words of the Testimony 186

AUDIO CD ORDER FORM 189

MESSIANIC REVELATION

Why the Tsiyon Interpretation of Revelation is SO Different!

There is little wonder why books on the Revelation prophecies abound today. Banks are failing, global markets are crashing, and global unemployment is rising; the harbingers of an ever-deepening global economic crisis. Volatile food and oil prices, food shortages, even food riots, underscore the crisis of survival now being faced by billions of the world's poor. War, rumors of war and an ever-increasing political and social divide ratchet up tensions. Disaster continues to brew in the Middle East. Enemies of Israel continue to menace her very existence from inside and out; while threatening to turn the whole world into a massive fireball. The seemingly endless man-made crises are also punctuated by a string of natural disasters and environmental anxieties. All these troubles and more, taken together, form an intractable tangle that has been termed "the world macro-problem."

Confronted with these escalating waves of global chaos Bible readers can't help but notice that this world situation fits the general pattern foretold in the Scriptures for the last days. We are witnessing the so called "signs of the times." As we see these signs, we're also seeing multiple predictions of the end of the world. It is not unusual to hear claims that the end is coming next month, next year, three years from now, five years from now. Multiple early dates are being predicted—each based on the same verses of Revelation.

In this climate of global anxiety, end-time speculation seems to be of interest to Bible believers and non-believers alike. Multiple doomsday theories abound from extra-Biblical sources: Peak oil, Planet X, the Mayan calendar, prophecies of Nostradamus, and of the Hopi Indians, to name a few. As one surveys the apocalyptic events of the 21st Century, while also being confronted with horrific predictions of our modern world sliced and diced a dozen different ways, it can all start to feel quite overwhelming.

THE BOOK OF REVELATION REVEALS OUR FUTURE

Knowledge is power. We have all heard that, because it's true. Imagine the advantage it would give you if you could know in advance what is really going on and why. Imagine the peace you would feel if you knew with certainty what is driving world events and where it is all headed. Then, you could be prepared in advance.

You really can know. YHWH (God's Name in Scripture) wants you to know. Everything having to do with this final generation that we are living in is foretold in the Scriptures. The best place to find the information you need to prevail through these last days is in the Book of Revelation.

Here, your response may be: "There are a million different interpretations of the Book of Revelation." True enough. Of course, that only adds to the confusion many people are experiencing regarding these chaotic days. Why am I adding yet another book on Revelation? Frankly, if I had no more to offer than all the others I would not have bothered to write this book.

A UNIQUE PERSPECTIVE ON REVELATION

What I'm offering here is a unique perspective on the Book of Revelation that is so fresh and so obviously true that it is nothing short of life-changing. This is what many of my radio listeners from over 65 countries have told me about this message after hearing it taught on my weekly radio series, *On the Road to Tsiyon*, in recent months. That series of radio programs predicted in advance the very changes that have now only recently started coming upon the world. Listeners who observed this happening saw this fulfillment as confirmation of the Revelation message they heard on the program. Based on the experience of so many of the listeners who have already heard this message, I can tell you what you can expect from this study. As we examine the Book of Revelation together, Revelation will be simplified for you. The approach we are taking to the Book of Revelation will help you to have a sense of certainty about it. You will know what it means.

It is really much simpler than the mountain of books and commentaries you may have studied in the past might have led you to believe. It is not that hard to understand the Book of Revelation—if only you start from the right frame of reference.

You see, most every other book on Revelation is written from a 21st Century Christian perspective, whether Dispensationalist, Supersessionist, Premillennialist, Amillennialist, Postmillennialist, or some variant or hybrid thereof. What is the problem with that? There were no 21st Century Christians when Revelation was written and neither were there any of the various theological constructs that drive Biblical interpretation today. Christian culture and theology of today was entirely unknown to the writer of Revelation. Not only because such did not exist then, but because, as you will learn in greater detail, the writer of Revelation was not "a Christian" in the sense that term is commonly understood today. There never was any such person as "Saint John the Divine" (Who is "Divine" besides the Almighty?). In fact, the writer of Revelation was a Messianic Jew who would have been horrified by such an idolatrous title. For that very reason Revelation would not be in your "New Testament" today, if some of its earliest enemies had their way.

Here is the truth of it. From about the 2nd Century forward Gentile Christians became evermore skeptical of all things Jewish, reflecting the anti-Semitic attitude of the Roman world generally. Thus abandoning the Hebrew roots of the faith, Greco-Roman believers developed a new religion which borrowed significantly from the ancient mystery religions and from Greek philosophy, the main influences from which Gentile converts sprang. This re-worked Gentile Christianity became so agreeable to the Roman mindset that in the 4th Century it was adopted as the State Religion. This produced the institution known from then forward as The Roman Catholic Church, the true mother of all Christian churches and denominations in the world today. Roman Christianity found it difficult to admit Revelation (the Apocalypse) as part of the "New Testament" precisely because it is so "Jewish." In the end, they had to include Revelation simply because it was already so fully established as authentic that they could not credibly do otherwise. As one scholar explained: "The only serious objection that can be urged against the authenticity of the Apocalypse, lies in the difference which is observable between its style, and that of the fourth Gospel. The latter is free from Aramaic expressions, the former is saturated with them." Further, "The Apocalypse bears, from one end of it to the other, the character of a Hebrew prophecy." (*Studies on the New Testament*, F.L. Godet)

Another Christian scholar comments on Revelation: "Though the language is Greek, the thoughts and idioms are Hebrew; and this links it on, not to the Pauline epistles, but to the Old Testament, and shows that its great subject is God's final dealings with the Jew and the Gentile; and not the Church of God." If we take "Church of God" to mean Gentile Christianity as explained above, and we take "Jew" as synonymous with Israel, as most Christian writers mean it, then it becomes self-evident that this statement is true. This scholar adds this remarkable comment: "It is undoubtedly written about the people of the Old Testament who are the subjects of its history. These will understand it as Gentile Christians can never hope to do." (*The Apocalypse*, E.W. Bullinger)

Given the utterly Hebrew character of the book, only a Messianic Jewish writer could have written the Book of Revelation. Having a Messianic Jewish writer, the Book of Revelation is itself a Messianic Jewish book. Unless you come to terms with the full implications of that fact you will never grasp the real meaning of the Book of Revelation.

Given this profound fact, your biggest challenge is sure to be setting aside mistaken theories you've heard about Revelation. All I ask is that you promise yourself to prayerfully consider this entire book you are reading before making your final decision about it, since one of its strongest proofs is the full, cohesive, picture it presents, building from the authentic foundation of Revelation that has been virtually ignored until now.

DIGGING IN TO REVELATION

Now let's dig right into the first chapter of Revelation. Revelation begins:

> This is the Revelation of Y'shua the Messiah, which God gave Him to show to His servants the things which must happen soon, which He sent and made known by His angel to His servant, Yochanan, who testified to God's word and of the testimony of Y'shua the Messiah, about everything that he saw. (Rev 1:1-2)

We are here using the *Hebrew Names Version* of the Bible. Using the original Hebrew names, though possibly sounding a little strange at first, will help you to see Revelation in its correct Hebraic historical and cultural context.

In the passage above we find paraphrased the title of the book we are studying: "The Revelation to Yochanan." Many people call the book "Revelations" with a plural "s" on the end. That's not correct. It is the Revelation (no "*s*") to Yochanan, who is more commonly known in English as John. The first verse says, *This is the revelation **of** Y'shua the Messiah.* Y'shua, not Jesus, is the actual Hebrew name by which Messiah was called by fellow Israelites with whom He lived all His earthly life. So it is the Revelation **to** Yochanan, but it is **of** Y'shua the Messiah. Where did Y'shua the Messiah get it?

The Revelation is that *which God gave Him.* As we continue on in the Book of Revelation, this order is evident over and over again. Father YHWH is the ultimate **Source** of all things. Things come to us from Him through Y'shua the Messiah. This chain of transmission moves forward from Messiah. Y'shua the Messiah transmitted His revelation through His angel to Yochanan. Then Yochanan wrote it all down so that eventually we could receive His revelation too. That Yochanan is informed by an angel, who in turn received this from Y'shua, Who received this from the Father, is all part of the revelation given to us.

THE PURPOSE OF REVELATION

Notice the purpose of Revelation. He gave it to *show His servants the things that must happen soon.* Are you one of His servants? Then Revelation was written for you. Some people say: "I don't read the Book of Revelation because it is too confusing for me." Father God gave this revelation to His servants so they would know the things that *must happen.* Since He wants you to know the things that *must happen* He can and will give you an understanding of His message by advancing the chain of transmission still further. I believe that's exactly what this book is about.

Here it says *the things which must happen.* Notice that word, **must**. None of this is going to be changed. It must happen! He wants you to know what must happen in advance. Why does He want you to know? He is a good Father who loves us. He wants us to be ready for the things that must happen.

In this Bible version it says, *things which must happen* ***soon***. Some Bibles translate that as *things which must happen* ***quickly***. The Greek word (G5034 *tachos)* translated as **soon** or **quickly** can mean "this is going to happen soon," as in the near future. It can't mean that here since we are now nearly two millennia since this revelation was given. That's not *soon* by any reckoning. The Greek word also has another meaning. It can mean **quickly** in the sense that, when something happens, it happens speedily as a rapid progression of events. This latter meaning is the correct meaning here. This overturns interpreters who tell you that the Book of Revelation is about the past two thousand years of "church history. " It's not. It's about things that are foretold to happen in rapid progression, with *the Lord's Day* as the focal point, at the end of the age.

IS "THE LORD'S DAY" SUNDAY?

I refer here to verse ten in which Yochanan states: *I was in the Spirit on* ***the Lord's Day***. What day is that? Many Christians writing on Revelation, and many more reading it, have assumed *the Lord's Day,* here referred to, is Sunday. It is natural for them to assume so, since it is the tradition of many generations of Christians to call Sunday "the Lord's Day." In this view, they think, John was worshiping on Sunday when he received the Revelation. However, they are quite mistaken regarding Yochanan's use of the phrase. The NT uses the phrase "first day of the week" but never uses "the Lord's day" in the same sense and "Sunday" not at all. As E. W. Bullinger, noted Anglican theologian, admitted: "There is no evidence of any kind that "the first day of the week" was ever called "the Lord's Day" before the Apocalypse was written. That it should be so called afterwards is easily understood, and there can be little doubt that the practice arose from the misinterpretation of these words." In other words, generations of Christians at sometime after Revelation was written lifted the phrase *the Lord's day* from the book of Revelation to apply it to their worship day, Sunday, though that was never the original meaning of the phrase. Bullinger further states: "It is passing strange that if John called the first day of the week 'the Lord's Day,' we find no trace of the use of such a title until a hundred years later which is the earliest date." (Mat 28:1, Mar 26:2,9, Luk 24:1, Joh 20:1,19, Act 20:7, 1Co 26:2, *The Apocalypse* by E.W. Bullinger)

All of that is to say: *the Lord's Day* of Revelation is the same as *the Day of the Lord* as spoken of through the mouth of the Hebrew prophets. Some may object here, supposing there is some difference in the two phrases, *the Lord's Day*, and *the Day of the Lord*, because we have *Lord's* used as an adjective in Revelation instead of as a noun in *of the Lord*, as in the Hebrew. However, there is no adjective for "Lord's" in Biblical Hebrew. In Hebrew to say "the Lord's Day" one must use the two nouns saying, "the Day of the Lord," making these two equivalent phrases. *The Lord's Day* in Greek is thus a perfectly acceptable translation of *the Day of the Lord* in Hebrew.

My point is this: when Yochanan said *I was in the Spirit on* ***the Lord's Day*** we can be sure he was not using that phrase to refer to Sunday–since that phrase would not be used to refer to Sunday until generations later. Rather, he was using the language of the Hebrew prophets. He was saying he was enraptured by the Holy Spirit in a prophetic vision of ***the Day of the Lord*** in a similar manner to the Hebrew prophets before him who had previously seen *the Day of the Lord* in the Spirit. It is a simple statement which informs us of the time period Revelation primarily treats. Revelation is about *the Day of the Lord* and its related events at the end of the age. (Isa 2:12, 13:6,9, Jer 46:10, Eze 13:5, 30:3, Joe 1:15, 2:1, 11, 31, 14, 3:14, Amo 5:18, 20, Oba 1:15, Zep 1:7,14, Zec 14:1, Mal 4:5)

YOCHANAN–AN EXHAUSTIVE WITNESS

Returning now to verse one and two, it mentions Yochanan, *who testified to God's Word and of the testimony of Y'shua the Messiah about everything that he saw.* He reported everything that he received in the Revelation. It's all included so there's nothing left out. That helps us to understand Revelation since we know there are no missing pieces. That is not to say that everything needed to interpret Revelation is included in Revelation. That's because Revelation often makes reference to other material outside of Revelation which it assumes readers already know. Revelation is written in something we could call "prophetic shorthand" whereby, if you know and understand the Prophets, just a couple of words in Revelation can draw multiple pages of that material into the Revelation message. In Yochanan's time all believers were well grounded in the prophetic Scriptures. Today most believers know very little about them, having relegated them to what they call "the Old Testament that was done away." Big mistake! We will be rectifying some of that for you with this book. Now, let's focus on the writer, Yochanan.

ESTABLISHING THE WRITER OF REVELATION

Who is this Yochanan? Some Bible critics say this was not the Yochanan known today as "Apostle John." They are wrong. The evidence against them is overwhelming. We have numerous witnesses from the time of living memory who testify to the fact that it was "John the apostle" that wrote the Book of Revelation.

Justin, who was a teacher in Ephesus, one of the assemblies that received the Revelation sent from Yochanan, is quoted very early in the 2nd Century, saying; "A certain man among us, whose name was John, one of the apostles of Christ, prophesied in a revelation made to him, that those who believed in our Christ would spend a thousand years in Jerusalem." (*Introduction to the New Testament*, Everett F. Harrison, page 455)

From those earliest days it was apparently common knowledge among believers that Yochanan, whom Greek speakers called *Ioannes apostolos*, i.e., *John the apostle*, prophesied the Revelation that reveals believers "will spend a thousand years in Jerusalem." Justin, an actual acquaintance of Yochanan, is thus our first witness. I would be persuaded by this witness alone, but there are more.

Irenaeus was a 2nd Century bishop who lived in the next generation after Revelation was written. That is very close to the actual writing of Revelation. He stated that men who saw John face-to-face personally certified the text of Revelation. In his own writings, Irenaeus repeatedly quotes from Revelation himself and accepts it as Scripture that was written by John the apostle.

Tertullian, a 2nd Century writer, agrees. He also quotes Revelation as Scripture and he too, holds John the apostle as the writer, and again, within the very next generation after Revelation was written.

Hippolytus was an early 3rd Century Christian writer. He also accepted Revelation as Scripture and he also accepted John the apostle as its writer.

With multiple witnesses who lived back then claiming John the apostle as the writer of Revelation, any critic speculating that the writer was not John the apostle must mightily prove his case. None of the critics can overcome these multiple witnesses. Yochanan, i.e., John the apostle, was the writer of Revelation.

RECEIVE THE BLESSING OF REVELATION!

> Blessed is he who reads and those who hear the words of the prophecy, and keep the things that are written in it, for the time is at hand. (Rev 1:3)

Revelation includes a blessing for reading it, hearing it, and keeping it. Here is another very good reason to read, hear, and keep the Book of Revelation. While Revelation concerns things which must happen, it also contains a lot of important instruction that has blessed believers of every age as they read and kept its instruction in their daily lives. Realize that, in one sense, the time is at hand for every believer. In other words, a thousand years ago the time was at hand because every single believer who is faithful to the end is going to be a part of these end-time events at the return of Y'shua. Thus, the time has always been at hand for all the believers who belong to Messiah and they will all be included in these end-time events.

FROM WHOM, TO WHOM, HEBRAIC GREETING

> Yochanan, to the seven assemblies that are in Asia: Grace to you and peace, from God, Who is and Who was and Who is to come; and from the seven Spirits who are before His Throne. (Rev 1:4)

The Book of Revelation is written as a letter (an epistle) like many of the other books included in the NT and it has a specific, immediate audience in mind, which in this case are the seven assemblies that are in Asia; more about them in the next chapter. We notice this letter has a greeting, *Grace to you and peace.* As with all of the epistles, Revelation has a greeting and an ending commensurate with a letter. The greeting further mentions, *God, Who is, Who was and Who is to come.* This last phrase is more correctly, *Who is to be.* This relates to the Hebrew Name of God, YHWH, which derives from the Hebrew verb that means "to be." It refers to Him as eternally to be; He was, He is, and He is to be. This is a reference to His eternal Name and Person as revealed to Israel. In other words, this is a classic Hebraic greeting.

Next, it mentions the seven Spirits who are before His Throne. Some people think that's seven angels because it mentions they're before the Throne. Others say it couldn't be angels because Yochanan wouldn't wish grace and peace to you from angels. That is true. In the prophetic Scriptures, we find the Spirit spoken of in terms of seven, speaking about the manifold presence of the Spirit. The Spirit is present everywhere, all the time. More about that later.

Y'SHUA THE MESSIAH, THE FAITHFUL WITNESS

> And from Y'shua the Messiah, the faithful witness, the firstborn of the dead, and the ruler of the kings of the earth. To Him who loves us, and washed us from our sins by His blood. (Rev 1:5)

Here is a good example of a prophetic book teaching doctrinal truth. We need to keep the Book of Revelation because it tells us who Y'shua the Messiah is. He's the *faithful Witness.* He faithfully witnesses to His Father, *Who is, Who was and Who is to be.* He faithfully witnessed unto death to His Father's Name. He's the firstborn from the dead. He went ahead for all of the rest of us that will follow Him. He *is the ruler of the kings of the earth* as He said, *All authority in heaven and on earth has been given to Me.* That's the position our Messiah is in, right now. He has all authority. *To Him Who loves us* reminds us what it means to be His. He gave His life for us and He *washed us from our sins by His blood.* We need to remember and keep that. (Mat 28:18)

A TORAH COVENANT PROMISE FULFILLED

> And he made us to be a Kingdom, priests to His God and Father; to him be the glory and the dominion forever and ever. Amen. (Rev 1:6)

He made us to be a Kingdom. That is past tense. We are made to be a Kingdom already. That's a point that's easily missed, because some make the mistake of thinking only of the Millennial Kingdom as the Kingdom. In the Millennial Kingdom, all persons will then be brought under the Kingdom. However, during this interim time since Messiah first came and set up the Kingdom, it's only those who accept Him as their Messiah and as their Savior that are transferred into the Kingdom, to function in His Kingdom in the earth today. This is why it says, *He made us to be a Kingdom, priests to His God."*

This language originates in the Torah ("the Pentateuch") where it is applied to Israel. In the Book of Malachi and then later in Peter, this is applied to the faithful remnant of Israel. This Kingdom phrase is from the Torah Covenant with faithful, believing Israel, and it's included right here at the beginning of Revelation. Here's another indication within these opening verses that Israel is a primary theme of Revelation. (Col 1:13, Exo 19:6, Mal 3:17, 1Pe 2:9; *Messiah Establishes His Kingdom,* On the Road to Tsiyon, Program #41, 10/06/2006)

THE COMING OF THE MESSIAH OF THE HEBREW PROPHETS

> Behold, He is coming with the clouds, and every eye will see Him, including those who pierced Him. All the tribes of the earth will mourn over Him. Even so, Amen. (Rev 1:7)

As we read this verse my mind is flooded with Scriptures from the Prophets referenced here as well as a number of verses in the NT. This includes prophecies from all through the Scriptures that talk about Him coming in the clouds, most notably, from the Book of Daniel. In the Book of Acts He ascended into heaven and was caught out of the vision of onlookers by a cloud. An angel said He will return in the same manner as He was seen ascending. (Dan 7:13, Act 1)

Every eye will see Him. He, Himself said as much. *For as the lightning flashes from the east, and is seen even to the west, so will be the coming of the Son of Man.* When He returns, all who are alive at the time will see Him. There is nothing in Scripture about an invisible return of Messiah to effectuate an invisible "rapture." Because the invisible "pre-trib rapture" doctrine is so prevalent today I hope to examine it in detail in a future volume. However, Revelation clearly does not teach such an invisible Return, since, when He comes back, *every eye will see Him,* including *those who pierced Him.* In saying *those who pierced Him,* this verse is specifically referring to those Israelites as mentioned in the Book of Zechariah, who upon seeing Him, will mourn with all the tribes of the earth that had rejected Him. (Mat 24:27, Zec 12:10)

THE GOD OF ISRAEL

> "I am the Alef and the Tav," says the Lord God, "Who is and Who was and Who will be, the Almighty." (Rev 1:8)

Here we're used to reading *I am the Alpha and the Omega.* In the Hebrew, it would be *the Alef and the Tav,* the first and last letters of the Hebrew alphabet. It's talking about the One Who is the Beginning and the End, the Eternal One, *the One Who is and Who was and Who will be,* once again referring to that revealed Name of YHWH, the Eternal: the God of Israel.

YOCHANAN, YOUR BROTHER IN TRIBULATION

> I, Yochanan, your brother and partner with you in tribulation, Kingdom, and perseverance in Messiah Y'shua, was on the isle that is called Patmos because of God's Word and the testimony of Y'shua the Messiah. I was in the Spirit on the Lord's Day, and I heard behind me a loud voice, like a shofar saying, "What you see, write in a book and send it to the seven assemblies: to Ephesus, Smyrna, Pergamum, Thyatira, Sardis, Philadelphia, and to Laodicea. (Rev 1:9-11)

Yochanan is explaining how he was directed to pass this revelation along to the seven assemblies named. He calls himself, *your brother and partner with you.* He's putting himself on the same level with them. That word (G2347 *thlipsis*) sometimes translated as *oppression* is better translated as *tribulation*, as we have restored it here. He's a partner with his intended hearers in *tribulation.* He's already mentioned that he and his intended hearers are made to be a Kingdom, so once again we have this same sense of the term. He, also, is persevering through troubles in Messiah Y'shua with them. Some Bible teachers today say believers should always be in "prosperity" and never have *tribulation.* Such have no need for *perseverance.* If they are right, how come we have this favored writer of the Book of Revelation who is *a partner...in tribulation*? Teachings that would spare modern day believers from tribulation tickle the ears of some, but they don't fit with Scripture or with real life. Neither do they fit with the history of what other faithful believers have gone through or are going through right now.

THE HEART OF YOCHANAN REVEALED

Notice that Yochanan wrote the Revelation on *the Isle of Patmos.* The Isle of Patmos still exists today. It's in the Aegean Sea. Patmos is not a very big island. It's about thirteen square miles. Today it has a population of about three thousand souls. In the 1st Century it was quite isolated. The Romans used Patmos as a penal island to banish undesirable persons; people that they thought weren't getting with the Roman program. Yochanan said he was sent there *because of God's Word and the testimony of Y'shua the Messiah.* The Romans were thinking they could shut him up by banishing him to Patmos. When is the last time you heard anything from them? That's right, never. By contrast, the Revelation written on Patmos has been read by countless millions, and continues to be read. God laughs at fools who think they can block His will.

Yochanan was calling Y'shua "Lord" rather than calling the Emperor "Lord." That was not well received in those days; hence, banishment to Patmos. Yet he did not whine about his troubles, as many of us might be given to do if removed from our homes and banished to some desolate island. Instead, he lived in blessed fellowship serving his Father in Heaven. He received the Revelation and wrote all of it down because he literally functioned as a bondslave of Messiah. Whatever happened in his life was accepted as part of his mission. He worked within his given circumstances to do the will of his Lord. That made him very useful and effective, even to you and I today. This is the unstoppable mindset of the overcomer.

Where did Yochanan get such tenacity? Certainly, having lived and walked in fellowship with Y'shua Messiah as one of His closest talmidim/disciples was unparalleled training–but there is more. This is a tenacity born of pure love. In fact, Yochanan was Y'shua's cousin and as such was His fast friend and "brother" since childhood. No doubt the two Jewish boys attended synagogue together on occasion and often shared together in the feasts and ceremonies of their rich Jewish culture as their respective families came together. As cousins and boys growing up together in Judea they knew each other in the way that only such boys can, having built a relationship to last a lifetime, and in this case, far beyond a lifetime. They were two Jewish boys who each did well for themselves. One became the rightful Messiah of Israel and the Savior of the world. The other knew it and believed it with all his heart and spent his entire life bearing witness to that truth. Yochanan was true to what he saw. He became a Messianic witness who has compelled millions to believe what he saw and experienced first hand. This is truth you can trust. (See *Y'shua's Family Album 3,* On the Road to Tsiyon, Program #6 02/11/06)

Messiah indicated that Yochanan would outlive the other apostles. This, in fact, he did. At the time of the Revelation he was of advanced years. With all he had done in his life for his One Great Cause, we might think that would have been enough. Yet, our Scriptures certainly would not be complete without the Book of Revelation. Way to go, Yochanan!

Yochanan says: *I was on the isle that is called Patmos,* and he says, *because of God's Word and the testimony of Y'shua the Messiah.* Then he explains, *while there, on Patmos, I was in the Spirit on the Lord's day."* That is, he was in the Spirit prophetically entering into the foretold *Day of the Lord* at the end of the age. Then he heard a voice behind him. *I heard a voice behind me* is an OT reference; *You'll hear a voice behind you saying, 'This is the Way, walk in it."* This is very Hebraic, as was Yochanan. The voice *is like a shofar* he said. A shofar, which is a trumpet fashioned from an animal horn, is sounded as an alarm. It means something important is about to happen. Again, this is a Hebraic connection. Then that voice said to him, *Write in a book and send to the seven assemblies* and it names those seven assemblies. (Joh 21:22, Isa 30:21)

WHEN REVELATION WAS WRITTEN AND WHY THAT MATTERS

There are two principle theories regarding when Revelation was written. Sometimes, you'll read that it was written shortly before the destruction of Jerusalem in 70 A.D., placing the writing in the 60s A.D. You'll also hear that it was written in the late 90s, about 95 or 96 A.D. The reason why you hear these two vastly different dates is because of the claims of pretorism, the theory that all of the prophecies of Scripture were finally fulfilled with the destruction of Jerusalem in the year 70 A.D. Pretorism requires that the prophecies of Revelation must have been written before 70 A.D. because Revelation talks about the *great tribulation* and other prophetic events as still future. Hence, Revelation fits the pretorist scheme only if written before 70 A.D. On the other hand, if the prophecies of Revelation were written in the 90s, long after 70, then pretorism is proven false. Pretorists just can't have Revelation still predicting a future *great tribulation* and other prophetic events long after all that is supposed to have been concluded! (Mat 24:21, Rev 7:14)

Unfortunately for the pretorists, it's well established in history when the Book of Revelation was written. Irenaeus, whom we mentioned earlier, from the next generation after the Book of Revelation was written, stated that it was written at the close of the reign of Emperor Domitian. This was also reiterated by a number of other early Christian writers. One of them is Victorinus. He was also a 2nd Century writer who lived close to the Domitian era, and he supports this same timing. We have this quote from him; "When John said these things, he was in the Isle of Patmos, condemned to the mines by Caesar Domitian. There he saw the Apocalypse; and when at length grown old, he thought that he should receive his release by suffering; but Domitian being killed, he was liberated." (*Introduction to the New Testament*, Everett F. Harrison, page 473)

It's very clear that Victorinus knew exactly what happened with John the apostle and knew details that we wouldn't know otherwise, including how it had all ended. Domitian was killed while Yochanan was still on the Isle of Patmos. Domitian reigned from 80/81 A.D. to 96 A.D. Jerusalem had already been destroyed for a decade by the time Domitian began his reign. By any account, Revelation could not have been written before the year 81 A.D., which is very bad news for the pretorists. Yochanan was still there after Domitian's death in 96 A.D. Therefore, it's well established that Yochanan actually wrote the Book of Revelation around 96. The Book of Revelation therefore points forward to the *great tribulation* and other prophetic events, most of which are still future. Many of these foretold events will be fleshed out in this book.

THE REVELATION IS "THOROUGHLY JEWISH"

Now that we have these fundamental facts laid out we return to the literary origin of the Book of Revelation. This is going to help unseal the Book of Revelation for you. While most Christian writers ignore the Hebraic origins of Revelation, I have quoted above from Christian scholars who are well aware of its Hebrew character. Now, let's read a quote from, of all things, the *Jewish Encyclopedia* to get the Jewish perspective. These are excerpts compiled from a lengthy article in the *Jewish Encyclopedia* on the Book of Revelation. This is especially interesting because, of course, the Rabbinic Jewish point of view does not accept the NT.

"Obviously, the writer of these visionary letters to the seven churches of Asia was in his own estimation a Jew, while believing in Jesus as the risen Messiah. He beheld him in his vision to be "the faithful witness" (martyr) who is next to God, "who is, was, and will be"... [Revelation]...contains several Jewish apocalypses worked into one...The whole apocalypse...is... in every part and feature...except where altered by the Christian compiler ...thoroughly Jewish in spirit and conception... It presents the development of the whole eschatological drama according to the Jewish view. It is Hebrew in composition and style, and bears traces of having originally been written in Hebrew." (Excerpts from *Jewish Encyclopedia-Revelation, Book Of*)

This is a fairly amazing quote. Most of us have always thought of the Book of Revelation as a "Christian" book. Perhaps surprisingly, Jewish scholars consider it a Jewish book. The *Jewish Encyclopedia* also says something else you may find amazing. It as much as states that the writer of Revelation was a Jew who believed in "Jesus" as the Messiah. If the book is "thoroughly Jewish" as this quote asserts, then it naturally follows that the writer of the book was "thoroughly Jewish" as well. Today it is considered a truism among Rabbinic Judaism that anyone who believes in "Jesus" as the Messiah cannot be a Jew. However, the *Jewish Encyclopedia* here indicates there has been at least one Jewish believer in Messiah and that was the writer of the Book of Revelation. Another very relevant fact from this quote is that the Book of Revelation contains "several Jewish apocalypses worked into one." We are told that "every part and feature is thoroughly Jewish in spirit and conception." How is this lightening bolt going to affect how we understand the Book of Revelation?

A HEBRAIC VIEW OF REVELATION

We need to understand Revelation in the context of its Hebraic roots. If we don't look at the Book of Revelation from a Hebraic standpoint, we will never understand it. If even unbelieving Jews recognize the Book of Revelation as a Jewish book, then certainly we should accept that as true. I'm not saying we must accept all of the claims made by the *Jewish Encyclopedia.* I reject the implications of the statement that the whole Apocalypse is Jewish "except for where it's been altered by the Christians."

There's no evidence that this claim of alteration is significantly true, though small translation differences did creep in over time. However, these are easy enough to ferret out by simple comparison with the earlier manuscripts. Such comparisons will inform our study later in this book. Even so, these tiny translation differences are normal and do not qualify as a significant alteration of the text. We've already considered the evidence as to who wrote it, when and where. Since the writer was an apostle of Messiah certainly everything that he wrote about Messiah was and is legitimately a part of the book. But, nevertheless, saying that Revelation is a "Jewish eschatological drama" and that "everything in it is Jewish in spirit and conception...its Hebrew in composition and style" is just amazingly telling.

The article says Revelation seems to have originally been written in Hebrew. How can this be known? It is really quite simple. Not only does Revelation reflect a Hebraic mindset in the ways already mentioned, but also it contains what are called 'Hebraisms.' In other words, it uses certain Hebrew phrases and expressions which are awkward when translated into Greek. These suggest that the book was originally written in Hebrew then translated into Greek. Yochanan likely wrote the Revelation in Hebrew, his mother tongue. He was also fluent in Greek as a secondary language, so likely did the translating into Greek himself. Since Greek was widely known throughout the Roman Empire, it is the Greek version that was widely distributed with multiple Greek manuscripts of Revelation surviving till now.

REVELATION–A JEWISH APOCALYPSE

In the very first verse of Revelation, it uses the word *revelation.* This is where the Book of Revelation gets its name. In Greek this is the word *apocalupsus.* In English that's *apocalypse.* In Greek this means "a disclosure or a revelation causing something to appear." This term, *apocalypse,* is also used to describe a certain type of Hebrew literature. You find this Hebrew literature, for example, in the OT. Books like Daniel and Ezekiel are examples of apocalyptic literature, in which you find visions and symbolism revealing future events. (Strong's Dictionary)

Most of us are much less familiar with other apocryphal Jewish writings that were transmitted in what's called *the intertestamental period.* In other words, after the OT was closed. These include books such as *The Book of Enoch, Jubilees, Esdras, The Assumption of Moses,* and so on. These books are part of the Hebraic heritage that influences the Book of Revelation. Most Christian interpreters have little to no knowledge of these books. Few Christians read these books, fewer still understand them. Many Christians either don't know or don't care that there are allusions to these books within the actual text of Revelation itself. This amounts to a huge blind spot so far as interpretation is concerned. Yochanan, being a Jew by birth, was familiar with all these books as part of his traditional Jewish education. Thus, allusions to all of these Jewish writings are included in the Book of Revelation. Even though they're not included in the Bible, they all share a connection with apocalyptic writings of the Prophets that are in the Scriptures.

JEWISH APOCALYPTIC GENRE IS PREDICTIVE OF THE FUTURE!

Something that is common to apocalyptic literature is that it all seeks to reveal hidden things about the future, usually about the end of this age and about the age to come. That's the standard for an apocalypse. Some people today talk about the Book of Revelation and say, "It's just talking about events that were going on back then. It's allegorical about events that go on in every age." Not taking a Hebraic view, they fail to realize that mere allegory is not the nature of apocalyptic literature, of which Revelation is a part. Jewish apocalyptic literature is predictive of the future! Revelation is no exception. It is the very pinnacle and capstone of all apocalyptic literature.

Certainly much that is true is always true, but that's not what apocalyptic literature is primarily about. It's about specific historical events that will happen. It's history in advance. The Book of Revelation, though containing truth that is relevant in every age, nevertheless, primarily reveals specific events, then future when written, having to do with the end of the age and the age to come. It is part of a certain genre of literature all of which has the same purpose and prophetic style. You can't arbitrarily break Revelation off and say it's something totally different than all the rest of the Jewish apocalyptic literature that it's part of, draws from and relates to. Yet, Christian interpreters routinely do that and we all let them get away with it. No more!

WHY EVERY INTERPRETATION YOU HAVE EVER HEARD OF REVELATION IS WRONG

Jewish apocalyptic literature, including that which is not in the formal canon, all descends or relates to the Prophets of the Hebrew Scriptures. That applies to Revelation even more than all of the other apocalyptic literature. In fact, the Book of Revelation refers back to apocalyptic symbols and references and phrases, from the OT Prophets, as well as from other apocalyptic literature and Hebraic sources, literally hundreds of times throughout the Book of Revelation. No less than 285 references to the OT have been identified by Christian scholars, who are clearly not seeing many more, while not seeing references to other apocalyptic literature at all. Typically, interpreters of the Book of Revelation ignore most or all of those Hebraic connections. Leaving all that out, it naturally follows that they arrive at a defective or deficient interpretation.

You really do have to take those Hebraic references into account in order to understand what Revelation is actually saying. In other words, you must come at the Book of Revelation from the same mindset as the writer of Revelation. That is a Hebraic-Messianic mindset. The Book of Revelation is not a Christian book. It's a Messianic Jewish apocalyptic book written by a Messianic Jew. Adopting that same mindset is a vital key to correctly interpreting the Book of Revelation.

Scary? Maybe.

Never fear. The book you are reading will help you deal with that daunting challenge.

THE TSIYON EXEGETIC APPROACH

This brings us to our final consideration of this first chapter, that is, our approach to the Book of Revelation. Ours is a literal, Hebraic, Messianic approach that is Ruach-led. This is the Tsiyon Interpretation.

Literal means that even though Revelation speaks in Hebraic apocalyptic symbols, the symbols point to real events that *must happen*. We must grasp the Hebraic symbolism while also recognizing that the symbolism refers to real facts and events. Our confirmation of this approach is found in the NT Scriptures themselves, because we have hundreds of prophecies from the Hebrew Prophets that the NT interprets as fulfilled by real facts and events in the life of Y'shua the Messiah. In the case of all those hundreds of prophecies, every single one of them was fulfilled by some real fact or real event. This is true of all of the prophecies of Scripture.

Hebraic means you can't divorce the Book of Revelation from the context of historic and actual Israel. This is something common to Jewish apocalyptic literature. Apocalyptic literature concerns itself with the plans and purposes of YHWH relative to Israel and the outworking of those plans and purposes for Israel at the end of the age and in the age to come. Israel is the axis around which all Hebraic prophecy revolves, so you can't throw Israel out of the picture or minimize Israel into a secondary or minor player. Think like a Hebrew.

Messianic means Revelation is written from the position that Y'shua the Nazarean is the Jewish Messiah from the House of David who was foretold by the Hebrew Prophets. Beyond that, Revelation sees Messiah as the principle Actor of the entire prophetic drama, having direct and intimate relationship with all who claim Him as their Lord. He is revealed as immediately available to all of the righteous, yet exercising absolute authority over both the world and the universal community of believers. Even more than being about Israel, Revelation is about Israel's Messiah to Whom Israel is forever inseparably linked. This is personal for me. I am blessed to be a bondslave of Messiah as was the writer of Revelation. It is therefore Messiah who commands my focus in the unfolding of this book you are reading, as in all aspects of my life. He alone is worthy!

The Ruach is the Hebrew term for the Spirit of YHWH. Revelation was inspired by the Spirit and can therefore only be understood with the aid of the Spirit. Let us acknowledge that we can never decipher Revelation like some sort of secret code that originates in the carnal mind of man. The Revelation has its source in YHWH! Only His Spirit can open our minds and hearts to its full and real meaning. Let us humbly seek the guidance of the Spirit of YHWH as we press on into the treasures of Revelation.

SEVEN ASSEMBLIES OF REVELATION

Revelation Chapters 1-3

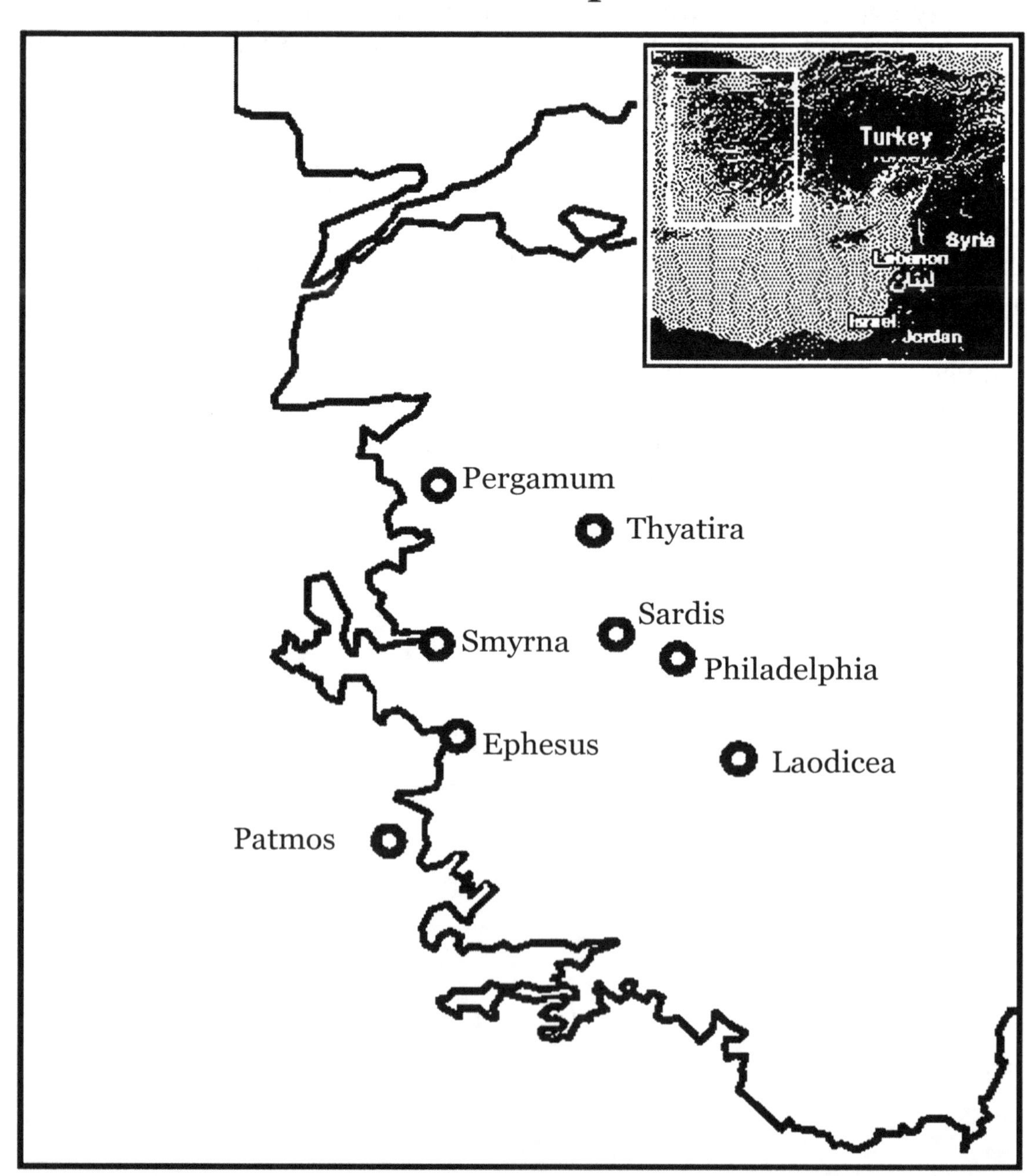

MESSIAH JUDGES HIS OWN

Messiah Revealed As Priest-Judge

The world will be judged..not believers. That is the popular idea today. However, that is not the Hebraic perspective of judgment. From a Hebraic perspective, it is characteristic of YHWH that Y'shua Messiah comes to judge His own in the very first chapter of Revelation.

MESSIAH COMES AS HIGH PRIEST

> I turned to see the voice that spoke with me. Having turned, I saw seven golden menorahs. And among the menorahs was One like a Son of Man, clothed with a robe reaching down to His feet, and with a golden sash around His chest. (Rev 1:12-13)

Here we have the *Son of Man clothed with a robe reaching down to His feet* and wearing *a golden sash.* He is seen in the midst of seven golden candlesticks or lampstands, as most commonly translated. Candlesticks or lampstands are not especially meaningful. However, when we look at this from a Hebraic perspective, as translated here in the HNV, we notice these are *seven golden menorahs.* Where do we find menorahs in the OT? This immediately suggests a connection with the menorahs of the Tabernacle and Temple of Israel.

A robe reaching down to His feet with *a golden sash* describes clothing of a priest. The golden menorahs provided the light inside the Temple. They were considered holy articles so that only a priest could set them in order. Each day a priest went into the Temple to tend the menorahs, along with the other Temple furnishings.This involved inspecting the menorahs, trimming the wicks, replacing the oil and generally taking care of the menorahs. Understanding this hebraically, we immediately see the

Son of Man among the seven golden menorahs acting as a Priest, there to tend the golden menorahs. (Exo 28, 25:31-40, 37:17-24, 39:37, Lev 24:4, 1Ch 28)

MESSIAH AS PRIEST-JUDGE JUDGES HIS OWN

> His head and His hair were white as white wool, like snow. His eyes were like a flame of fire. His feet were like burnished brass, as if it had been refined in a furnace. His voice was like the voice of many waters. He had seven stars in His right hand. Out of His mouth proceeded a sharp two-edged sword. His face was like the sun shining at its brightest. When I saw Him, I fell at His feet like a dead man. (Rev 1:14-17)

All of the figures here are drawn out of the Hebrew Scriptures. For example, in the Book of Daniel, YHWH judges from His Throne with *hair white like wool* and *like snow.* The Hebrew Prophets display YHWH with fire coming forth from His Throne. Brass was the metal used for the laver in which the priests washed themselves to prepare for their Temple service. The phrase *feet like burnished brass* therefore refers to Messiah's walk of absolute and perfect righteousness. *A voice like many waters* is heard above all else. We must hear His voice. *A sharp two-edged sword* cuts both ways. The judgments out of His mouth perfectly divide good from evil and give to each one appropriately, according to their works. All these are symbols of divine judgment. This is why He is in the midst of the menorahs. He has come as Priest-Judge. This is appropriate since a priest judges the people. His appearance coming in judgment is so fearsome that when Yochanan saw Him "*he fell on his face like a dead man.*" (Dan 7:9-10, Eze 1, Exo 30, Psa 149:6-9, Heb 4:12, Deu 17:8-13)

After uplifting Yochanan with a reassuring touch and a reminder that He is the First and the Last, the Living One with the keys to death itself, Messiah identifies the seven menorahs. (Rev 1:17b -19)

THE SEVEN MENORAHS

> The mystery of the seven stars which you saw in My right hand, and the seven golden menorahs. The seven stars are the angels

of the seven assemblies. The seven menorahs are the seven assemblies. (Rev 1:20)

THE SEVEN MENORAHS ARE THE SEVEN ASSEMBLIES

These assemblies are named as Ephesus, Smyrna, Pergamum, Thyatira, Sardis, Philadelphia, and Laodicea. These assemblies were located in the Roman Province of Asia Minor in the area of modern day Turkey, within traveling distance of the Land of Israel. Many of the disciples of those assemblies were Jews, since there was a large Jewish community emanating out from the Land of Israel. That was especially true after the destruction of Jerusalem, when many of the Judeans were dispersed. In each of these congregations there were also Gentile believers who had joined themselves to the Jewish believers.

These seven assemblies are listed in the natural traveling order of the circuit needed to distribute this letter to the seven assemblies. Once the letter arrived at a given assembly, it then went out from there to other assemblies. Each of these original assemblies thus served as a publication point for the letter, until it finally reached well beyond the original seven assemblies.

The blessing that we read in Revelation 1:3 is one indication of this. It says, *Blessed is he who reads and those who hear the words of the prophecy, and keep the things that are written in it.* In every synagogue, there was a **shaliach** (messenger) who read the word to the congregation. This was true among the Messianic congregations as well. *Blessed is he who reads* was directed to the shaliach who read the letter in each of the assemblies. *And those who hear the word of the prophecy* refers to the persons in the congregations who heard it read. This order indicates the process with which the Revelation was to be spread in the various assemblies, and from there to many other assemblies, right down to us today.

The admonition to the seven assemblies takes up only the first three chapters of this book of 22 chapters. The admonition for the seven assemblies in the first three chapters got the Revelation circulated and widely distributed so that we, the ultimate intended recipients, would have it now, at the end of the age.

The seven assemblies in Asia Minor are seven golden menorahs. What is a menorah for? The menorah gives off light. The purpose of an assembly is to shine forth the Light of Messiah. Assemblies are therefore menorahs. (Exo 35:14, Num 8:2, Mat 5:14)

THE SEVEN STARS

Messiah says the *seven stars in His right hand* are the *seven angels of the seven assemblies.* The Greek word here translated as **angel** (*ang'-el-os*) means **messenger**, whether spirit or human. This isn't talking about spirit beings in this case. It's talking about ***the messenger of the assembly*** to whom the message to each respective assembly is entrusted. Letters need not be sent to spirits, but are sent to men. Every assembly of believers was structured after the structure of ancient Israel. In ancient Israel, in every town, there was a body of elders who were responsible for the government of the town and there was one among the elders who was the leader. He was called the **nasi**. He was the prince of the elders. He served as **president** of the body of elders with the final responsibility falling upon him. Among the assemblies of early believers the president of the elders was deemed *the messenger of the assembly.* He was the one responsible to receive this Revelation message and to see it was conveyed to the assembly as well as to lead in its implementation. As such he was like a star in the right hand of Messiah, to carry out His will. (Rev 2:1, 8, 12, 18, 3:1, 7, 14)

Now, let's put this picture all together. We see the resurrected and exalted Messiah coming as High Priest, walking in the midst of the menorahs, tending to the menorahs, judging them. He has the seven stars in His right hand, in His direct control. Messiah is thus in control of the messengers of the assemblies, who speak for Him. With this picture Revelation begins with Messiah judging—not the world—but His own.

JUDGMENT MUST ALWAYS COME TO GOD'S OWN FIRST

While judgment of God's own violates modern Christian theology, it is clearly the picture we find here. From the Hebraic point of view, judgment must always begin with the House of God. Only after that does judgment go out to the world. YHWH judges His own first and then He judges the rest of the world, as He himself indicates.

> For behold, I begin to work evil at the city which is called by My name...for I will call for a sword upon all the inhabitants of the earth, says YHWH of hosts. (Jer 25:29)

Here in Jeremiah the judgment begins *on the city which is called by His name* and that city, of course, is Jerusalem. Jerusalem has been destroyed in the past by the judgments of YHWH. After that He judged the offending nations.

JUDGMENT ON THE HOUSE OF GOD IN THE NT

Perhaps you've been told things are different in the "New Testament?" Not according to Kefa/Peter the apostle. He said:

> **Judgment <u>must</u> begin at the house of God**: and if it first begin with us, what shall the end be of them that obey not the good news of God?" (1Pe 4:17 KJV, emphasis added)

Peter, being Jewish, understood this principle. Peter, unlike many believers today, expected judgment on the House of God first. He asked, "if it's going to start with us, how will it be for those who do not obey the good news?" Apparently Peter felt that the House of God <u>is</u> obeying the good news, since a contrast is being made here with those who do not obey. Even so, there must be judgment on the House of God. How so?

JUDGMENT MAY BE FOR OR AGAINST

The word here translated as *judgment* is the Greek word ***kree-mah***. It means **a decision for or against.** It doesn't necessarily have a negative connotation, as the word *judgment* generally does in English. It is more like what happens when you are facing a job assessment. Your boss may say, "You're doing great!" He may point out a few changes you need to make or he may even fire you. If you are judged or, in other words, assessed by

Messiah, He sees the positive and He sees the negative. Peter is saying that this kind of judgment or assessment must start with the House of God and then it goes out from there.

When Messiah comes as the High Priest to judge the seven assemblies, that judgment is not necessarily negative. It could be, since these are judgments for or against. This is what the Scriptures speak of as *righteous judgment.* It is prophesied in the Hebrew Prophets that Messiah will judge with righteous judgment. That's what's happening here.

On seeing the seven assemblies being judged we might breathe a sigh of relief thinking, "Well, I'm glad it's them and not us." To do that would be premature because the judgment regarding these seven assemblies points forward to the greater judgment at the end of the age. That greater judgment must follow the same pattern, starting with God's own household before going on to judge the world. This truth finds growing support as we continue on in Revelation. (Heb 10:30)

A DUAL FULFILLMENT OF THIS REVELATION PROPHECY

Messiah as our great High Priest speaking to Yochanan, says:

> Write therefore the things which you have seen, and the **things which are**, and the **things which will happen** hereafter. (Rev 1:19, emphasis added)

In these words, Messiah shows us that the things He is saying and showing Yochanan are about the *things which are.* In that context, *the things which are* pertain to the seven actual assemblies that are spoken of in Revelation. They existed at that time. The Revelation message went out to those seven assemblies and was relevant to those seven assemblies then.

Messiah also says *things which will happen hereafter.* There is a future fulfillment *hereafter.* Thus, there are two fulfillments of these Revelation messages to the assemblies. The first fulfillment was on those actual seven assemblies. The fulfillment *hereafter* is the fulfillment that occurs on all of the assemblies in the last days, before the return of Messiah. We know

Revelation is talking here to the end-time generation because as we read through these first three chapters of Revelation, we find frequent references to end-time events in which the believers are warned, for example, to be awake and paying attention at the coming of Messiah. Other last days references abound, all confirming that the fulfillment *hereafter* is in the last days. The signs are all around us that we are in those last days now. By grasping the meaning of Messiah's judgment on the seven assemblies we can better understand the meaning of these chapters of Revelation as they apply to us today.

STRUCTURE OF THE JUDGMENTS OF THE SEVEN ASSEMBLIES

After prayerfully reading the first three chapters of Revelation, let's examine the structure of these judgment messages of Messiah together. You will find common elements throughout.

- **Judgments of commendation**, if any, are the words you want to hear.

- **Judgments of sin**, if any, are forthrightly stated. Some of the things that Messiah has judged believers as guilty of are very, very serious sins, not just sins that are a mistake or are an omission.

- **Judgments of punishment** follow, when believers commit willful sins and they don't repent. There are negative consequences when a believer continues down a path he or she should not be on. First, there's the warning. Then, if the believer continues on that path of willful sin, the punishments stated will happen.

- **Judgments of reward** are offered, for those who repent of sin or those who continue on without falling into sin, in other words, for the overcomers. Those happy judgments for the overcomers are amazing!

This begs the question: Are these judgments for the assemblies as a whole or do they also apply to individuals? While there are certain trends and tendencies in certain assemblies, Y'shua always rewards the overcomers. **Overcomers are individuals that rise above sin.** It is not whole assemblies that receive the rewards as overcomers, but those people from within the assemblies who actually overcome. In fact, all **of the rewards go to the overcomers.**

One last common element emerges. At or near the close of each message, we always find these words; *he who has an ear let him hear what the Spirit says to the assemblies.* This statement appearing with each judgment message shows that those messages have a wider application beyond those seven assemblies, since everyone who *will hear* is told to pay attention to the messages given to these seven assemblies. For this reason believers living in the last days are rightly held responsible to obey.

Here is a summary of the judgments of the seven assemblies.

JUDGMENTS OF COMMENDATION IN THE ASSEMBLIES

- Toil
- Perseverance
- Discernment and shunning of apostates and false apostles
- Endurance in His name
- Not weary of doing good
- Hate for works of priestcraft (Nicolaitans)
- Endured tribulation
- Endured temporal poverty
- Endured blasphemy of false Jews
- Hold firmly to His name
- Didn't deny the faith under persecution
- Works
- Love
- Faith
- Service
- Patient endurance
- Increase of works over time
- Undefiled garments of holiness

DO COMMENDATIONS OF MESSIAH REFLECT YOUR BEHAVIOR?

The list of judgments of commendation reflects a Hebraic mindset, though running contrary to the modern Christian mindset. For example the first commendation in Revelation is for **toil**. Hard work! That's a "works mentality" you say? Wait a minute. It is Messiah Himself who holds *toil* as a positive value. Toil is actually a Hebraic value and is expected of believers. Messiah has every right to expect you to work hard to produce fruit for His Kingdom.

Not convinced? Read the list again. Messiah specifically commends industrious ones for their **works**. He also commends **love**, **faith**, **service**, **patient endurance** and an **increase of works over time**. In other words, not only continuing to do works but **doing more and more works!** As a believer becomes stronger in the faith, as more time passes, the believer should be doing more works all the time, carrying a greater load of works, if you will. Once again, we see Messiah having a very different attitude than the modern prevailing view of works. All of the values we find here are much more Hebraic than Christian, using *Christian* in the sense of modern Christian norms.

It gets worse. There's a school of thought today amongst some believers that if you have *tribulation* in your life, you must have done something wrong. However, Messiah commends believers for **enduring tribulation** and for **enduring poverty**. Why would Messiah allow some believers to have **tribulation**, have **poverty**, have **toil**, and need to **persevere** and have **endurance**? What is all this about?

All of these commendations go to virtues having to do with the perfecting of our character. In other words, in Messiah's judgment it is not enough for us to have righteousness imputed to us through His blood without righteousness being actualized in our lives. He expects us to grow in righteousness to become actual righteous people! **Righteousness** is one of the highest Hebraic values.

This is confirmed in that some of those believers were commended for their **undefiled garments of holiness.** If that was merely speaking of the holiness imputed to all believers, then why commend anyone for it? The commendation is given to overcomers because they actually live out real **holiness**. They live holy (set-apart) lives.

Another commendation that displays a Hebraic mindset involves Messiah's hatred of *the works of the Nicolaitans.* This word actually includes the Greek word for *laity.* It refers to the clergy/laity distinction or priestcraft that crept in among some early believers and eventually grew until it swallowed up the Gentile Church. Messiah commends those who **hate priestcraft**.

JUDGMENTS OF SIN IN THE ASSEMBLIES

- Left first love
- Mixing of true worship with paganism and sexual immorality (balaam)
- Priestcraft (Nicolaitans)
- Toleration of Jezebel
- Dabbling in deep things of satanic spiritualism
- Hypocrisy
- Spiritual death
- Unperfected works
- Luke-warmness
- False assessment of being rich
- Spiritual blindness to own wretched condition

MESSIAH JUDGES SINS OF BELIEVERS

Have you been taught that because of grace Messiah only sees the good things you do? That He just blots out and doesn't see any of the bad things you do? Here in the Book of Revelation, there are lots of behaviors in the assemblies that He saw and judged as sin. There's a long list and each sin on that list should be carefully considered. We have space here to only include a sampling.

Left the first love–I wonder how many of us really understand that is **sin**. You come on strong and then over time your love for Him wanes. You might even think: "Well, I'm saved now, so now I can get on with what I really want to do. He's going to love me anyway." He judges that attitude as sin.

Mixing of true worship with paganism and with sexual immorality—He judged them for that. **Priestcraft** is again named, as is the **toleration of Jezebel**. This has to do with a spirit of feminist domination and witchcraft. This often involves a self-assumed prophetess in the assembly. This also includes a libertine pseudo-spirituality that allows for sexual immorality and an anti-Torah, anti-righteousness mentality.

Spiritualism, general **hypocrisy, spiritual death**–having the name of being alive in Messiah but really being dead, being just **lukewarm**, going through the motions, thinking that you've got it all when you really don't have anything. All of these are considered very serious sins with very serious consequences.

Messiah confronts believers directly for all of these sins. *His eyes are like a flame of fire.* He sees everything and exposes it all to the light. This is our Hebraic Messiah. (Rev 2:18)

JUDGMENT OF REWARDS TO "HIM WHO OVERCOMES"

Overcomers:

- Will be rewarded with entrance into Paradise to eat from the Tree of Life.
- Will have exemption from the second death.
- Will receive hidden manna, which is hidden truth from above.
- Will receive a white stone with a new name, which is a unique acceptance and identity known in relationship with God alone.
- Will receive authority over the nations in the Kingdom.
- Will receive the Morning Star, which is personal intimate fellowship with Messiah forever.
- Will receive white garments of perfect righteousness.
- Will receive a permanent name in the Book of Life, which is immortality.
- Messiah will confess the overcomer in heaven before YHWH and the angels.

- Will be a pillar in the Temple without end.
- Will have the Name of God written upon him.
- Will have the name of the New Jerusalem written upon him.
- Will have the new name of Messiah written upon him.
- Will sit down on the Throne with both the Son and the Father!

BE AN OVERCOMER!

Carefully consider the rewards that will go to the overcomer. They are all wonderful, but I will only comment here on the last one. The overcomer will not be given a throne. Messiah says the overcomer *will sit on My Throne with Me and My Father!* I dare not even write out the outrageously magnificent implications of such a reward. These are the rewards that will come to the overcomers. There is no reward better than this. That's one reason my entire life's goal is to be an overcomer. How about you?

WHAT IS AN OVERCOMER?

The apostate church would have you believe that all of these rewards will be given to every believer, no matter what they do. On the contrary, Messiah says that to receive these rewards you must be an overcomer. What must you overcome? The context makes this answer crystal clear. Overcomers are the opposite of unrepentant sinners. They overcome sin, the world, and the devil. Grace is given, not only that we might have forgiveness, but more importantly, that we might overcome.

Let me paint you a picture of what we're talking about here. Through the course of your walk with Messiah, you're going to have trials and troubles and difficulties thrown at you. Sometimes you're going to do well overcoming such trials and temptations in faith. Sometimes you're going to fail. However, when the overcomer fails he then repents and overcomes. An overcomer is not necessarily somebody who never does anything wrong. He is a person who always recovers if he does something wrong, and then goes on to overcome. The end of every struggle for him is victory over sin. The overcomer prevails to the very end. Thus prevailing, the overcomer secures the reward.

HOW OVERCOMERS RECEIVE THE REWARDS

All of these rewards are the judgments for the overcomer and they're really wonderful. Some of them are rewards to be received in the age to come, but some of them are received in this age. For example, we have the reward of having the Name of God and of Messiah written on the overcomer. Later in the Book of Revelation we find overcomers on Mount Tsiyon (Zion) who are seen having the Name of God and Messiah written on them. Thus, some rewards come to overcomers even in this life, but, by far, the majority of the rewards will come to the overcomers in the eternal state. These rewards don't come to you only because Messiah died for you. Messiah's death for the believer secures his salvation, but the rewards of the overcomer go far beyond mere salvation. If you want to be an overcomer, you must be very serious about all the judgments of Messiah in these three chapters of Revelation and must learn to obey Him in all things. (Mat 7:21-27)

Why am I telling you this? My goal is exactly the same as Messiah's goal in Revelation chapters 1-3. I want to encourage believers to obtain a right assessment of themselves so that they can go on to grasp this prize that will come to overcomers, realizing one must toil to get there. These rewards aren't going to come to anyone who is lazy about his or her spiritual life. This is very clear from these words in Revelation. These rewards are only going to be given to people who, in a relative sense, have earned it. Of course I know that ultimately none of us can *earn* eternal life. I'm not saying that you can earn your salvation. Here in Revelation chapters 1-3 it is speaking of a relative type of earning something. (Phl 2:12, 3:11-15, 1Co 9:24-27)

PARABLE OF THE OVERCOMERS

The Kingdom of Heaven is like this: Imagine that by some strange burp of the universal space-time continuum you have been stranded on a desolate planet millions of light-years from earth. You have absolutely no hope of getting yourself home. You are doomed. Realizing your completely hopeless condition you cry out to Messiah for help. He hears you and has pity on you, then snaps His fingers and you materialize on your living room couch in New Jersey. You have just been saved. Now, what are you going to do with that salvation? Spend it on your own selfish interests and you are still saved—but you are wasting your salvation. Respond in gratitude by serving Messiah and your fellowman with your whole heart and you are giving evidence that you are more than just saved—you actually are worthy of saving. You are an overcomer. Messiah is pleased with your worthy response, so rewards you by making you king of New Jersey. Did you save yourself? No. Only Messiah could do that. Did you prove yourself worthy once saved? Hey, Messiah made you king of New Jersey! (Mat 5:20, 8:11-12, 25:1-46, 2Pe 2:20-21)

GRASP THE PRIZE!

Getting a reward for overcoming means you did something to merit the reward. What you do results in the reward in the sense that, if you don't behave as an overcomer the reward will not be yours. Study this out, starting with the verses cited herein. Examine your life. Do you see that Messiah comes as the High Priest in the midst of the assemblies, to judge His own? Then if you want to be an overcomer invite that judgment now. Seek Him and seek His help to make the changes in your life that are needed so that you will be counted among the overcomers. In a sense, to do anything less than seeking His judgment, even of our weaknesses as well as our strengths, is spiritual laziness. You can be judged now or later. Judgment must come to us all eventually. Willingly receive it now that you might receive the reward of the overcomer then! (Mat 11:12, Joh 16:33, Eph 2:1-10, Heb 10:26-31, 1Co 3:11-15, 1Pe 4:5)

JUDGMENTS OF PUNISHMENT AGAINST BELIEVERS

Making *war against them with the sword out of His mouth* includes:

- Exposure of evil deeds
- Serious sickness
- Death of their children
- Great tribulation
- He will come as a thief at a time they do not know

UNREPENTANT SINNERS ARE PUNISHED!

Much of this is shocking in the light of modern day toleration of sin among believers. We don't think of Messiah as making war against any of us. We think of Him as making war against unbelievers. Yet He's speaking here of making war against the sinners in the assemblies who don't repent. He says **He's going to *war against them with a long sword out of His mouth*,** exposing their evil deeds.

We might not believe that serious sickness can come upon believers because of their sins. Yet, here in Revelation, Messiah says exactly that. Here we are told serious sickness can result from spiritual laxity and/or serious sin, especially having to do with *sexual immorality* and *idolatry*. ***Messiah says those same sins, if not repented of, can bring on a person's death or even the death of their children.*** If anybody understands the Torah, then they will understand this. If they don't understand the Torah, then they are without sufficient measure to understand these consequences of evil behavior.

Another punishment mentioned here is ***great tribulation***. This term is used later in Revelation referring to the coming great tribulation at the end of the age. Believing, unrepentant, sinners will not be spared from the affects of the great tribulation. If believers continue in the sins Messiah lists in these three chapters, then they can expect to share in the same plagues and punishments as the unbelieving wicked during the great tribulation. That is a good reason to seek Him for His judgment of our own lives before the evil day comes. (Rev 18:4)

The last punishment listed here occurs when **Messiah *comes as a thief at a time they do not know*.** The apostate church says that believers won't know when Messiah is coming. They call this the *Doctrine of Imminency*. Here in Revelation we learn that <u>not</u> knowing the time of His coming in advance will be a punishment upon "believing" sinners. Of course, this suggests that as they get closer to the time of His coming, the righteous will know in advance when He's coming. His Return **will not** fall upon the righteous as a thief.

We have already mentioned the multiplication of dates being projected for His Return. The sheer number of those dates, all different, indicates that many today are in sin, because all those dates, all those projections to which various camps hold, can't all be correct. By contrast, the overcomers will not need to speculate because they will <u>know</u> the time of His coming in advance. Yet another reason why we should be overcomers!

JUDGMENTS OF PUNISHMENT AGAINST ASSEMBLIES

- Menorah moved out of its place
- I will vomit you out of my mouth, i.e., a rejection and removal of these assemblies

UN-REPENTED SIN BRINGS PUNISHMENT TO THE ASSEMBLIES

Now we get to another category of judgment by the High Priest in the midst of the menorahs. These are the judgments of punishment against the unrepentant assemblies. There are certain punishments that are listed against individuals, which we have discussed above. Then there are also punishments that are listed against the unrepentant assemblies themselves.

A *menorah moved out of its place* is an assembly that loses its witness and is uprooted and removed from service. This doesn't happen by accident or bad luck. When an assembly is removed from its place, it is the High Priest in charge of the menorahs that has removed that assembly.

I will vomit you out of My mouth is an even stronger way of saying the same thing. If an assembly is not showing forth the light as Messiah wishes it to be shown He is perfectly capable of removing that assembly from its place *and* from His service. (Rev 3:16)

WHAT BECAME OF THE SEVEN ASSEMBLIES?

All of the original seven assemblies were, in fact, entirely removed from their place. At the time of the Revelation, there was a Greek speaking population in Asia Minor. As we've said, Asia Minor was a Roman province located in modern day Turkey. This is the area where the original seven assemblies of Revelation were located. Greek-speaking assemblies in that area eventually were assimilated into the Greek Orthodox Church. The actual descendants of the Revelation assemblies of Asia Minor continued to occupy that area down into the modern age until 1923.

Answers.com summarizes what happened then: "The Seven Churches of Revelation, also known as The Seven Churches of the Apocalypse and The Seven Churches of Asia (referring to the province of Asia, not the continent), are seven major churches of Early Christianity, as mentioned in the New Testament Book of Revelation. All seven sites are in modern-day Turkey and no longer have significant Christian populations since they were emptied of Christians under the Treaty of Lausanne." (http://www.answers.com/topic/seven-churches-in-asia)

In 1923, the *Treaty of Lausanne* provided for a mass removal of all of the Greek Orthodox Christians from the areas of Turkey here under discussion. As a result all remnants of the original seven churches were removed out of Turkey in 1923. They were moved out of their homes, out of their cities, out of the country. They were cleared out after living in the same area for at least two millennia.

Some didn't go at first. Turkey established laws against them, levied special taxes that only applied to the Christians, and applied pressure until the rest of them eventually left also. There were over two million of these Greek Orthodox Christians in Turkey previously. This number was reduced to possibly as few as two thousand Christians in all of Turkey today. These remaining few have no visible presence at all.

The seven assemblies have had their menorahs removed, even as Messiah warned in the Book of Revelation. Note that this fulfillment literally happened and it happened within memory of some people still living today. Their menorahs were removed in compliance with an agreement, by the way, that was made with the Greek Orthodox Church. This was a religious thing, not just an ethnic thing. When I learned of this fulfillment of Messiah's words, I was amazed. I shouldn't have been amazed. The Scripture foretold it and all Scripture must be fulfilled.

All of this has grave implications for believers here in this final generation and we do well to consider those implications in detail; more about that in the next chapter.

MESSIAH JUDGES HIS OWN-AGAIN

Last Days Judgment of the House of God

In the previous chapter we learned that the seven assemblies of Revelation chapters 1-3 were literally removed from their place, just as Messiah said would happen if they did not repent. This literal fulfillment is part of that message for us. The literal removal of the menorahs, the seven assemblies, is actually a prophetic-type of the final fulfillment of Revelation chapters 1-3 in the last days, part of *the things that must happen hereafter* that Messiah spoke of in His introduction of Revelation. Those seven assembles represent the whole end-time church system in these last days. That's not good news for the church system today. The removal of those seven churches in fulfillment of Messiah's words suggests that the end-time church system must also experience removal of their menorah, their witness, and light of Messiah. Why is that so? For all the same reasons Messiah ultimately judged against the original seven churches.

SINS OF THE CHURCH SYSTEM JUDGED BY MESSIAH

Here is a list of sins judged by Messiah against the seven churches—as applied to the modern church system.

- **Paganism and satanic spiritualism** are the source of many of the rites practiced in the church system today. Look up Christmas, Easter, Halloween and the religious symbols and rites commonly used by churches in your encyclopedia. You will find a plethora of pagan and satanic connections there.

- **Hypocrisy?**–The modern church system is known for hypocrisy.

- **Spiritual death?** –Have you ever been in a dead church? How about a live one?

- **Unperfected works?** –That could be the motto of the modern church system.

- **Lukewarm-ness?** –Most believers don't even warm a seat in their church anymore.

- **False assessment of riches?** –Wealthy churches abound. Truly rich churches are rare.

- **Spiritual blindness?** –The church system fails to see all of this.

GOD DOESN'T JUDGE WITH FAVORITISM

Clearly, righteousness demands that the sins listed in Revelation against the seven churches apply with equal or greater force to the modern church system. If actual history shows the punishment that befell the seven churches for these very sins was the removal of their menorah—the actual removal of their light of Messiah—then what must be the outcome for the modern day church system guilty of the same sins? This is not rocket science. The outcome must be the same upon the last-days church system according to the divine standard of righteous judgment since *God doesn't show favoritism.* (Act 10:34)

Given these facts, what Revelation 1-3 suggests to us, is that the end-time church system that has come down to us to this day, like those seven churches, must also have its menorah removed. This means the removal of its place of witness for Messiah in this world.

RAPTURED OR REMOVED?

Many church people today believe "the church" can be removed only by a 'pre-tribulation rapture of the church' whereby their church, and they themselves, will be snatched out of harm's way. However, we are learning here that the removal of the apostate church system from its place is not going to be by a pre-tribulation rapture as many today mistakenly imagine. They think that their church system can continue on in all of the sins listed in Revelation, and many more, and still be raptured away to the favor and presence of God. That is a deception; a mere illusion that flies in the face of the judgments of our High Priest. (Mat 25:1-13, Rom 11:19-21, Note: A detailed refutation of the pre-trib rapture doctrine will be included in a future volume.)

ALL WHO PROFESS BELIEF IN MESSIAH INCLUDED

We've seen that Revelation chapters 1-3 depict Messiah as our High Priest walking in the midst of the seven churches, judging them. We've also seen that the seven churches represent all assemblies/churches professing belief in Messiah/Christ in the last days. Some have asked: How do we know that these judgments include all last-days assemblies, including the false ones? Wouldn't Messiah only be concerned with churches/assemblies approved by Him?

Look again at the context of the first three chapters of Revelation. The practices mentioned include things like heresy, idolatry, sexual immorality, and even satanism. Are those practices things that you expect to find in churches/assemblies that are approved by Messiah? No. You wouldn't find those practices among people that are truly following Messiah. The picture here is therefore a judgment of all Christ-professing churches, not just the ones that are approved. After all, the point here is to separate out those overcomers who are approved from all the people that claim to be professing Messiah but who, in fact, are found to be unworthy. (Mat 3:10)

JUDGMENT MADE MANIFEST

To all of those persisting in these various sins Messiah has this word:

> Repent therefore, or else I am coming to you quickly, and I will make war against you with the sword of My mouth. (Rev 2:16)

This is very serious when we understand that Messiah is actually making war in the midst of the assemblies. "*The sword of My mouth*" suggests a special kind of punishment, that is, punishment by the Word, since it's coming out of the mouth. This includes exposure of sins. Sins in the church system that are kept hidden are hereby exposed to public knowledge. Do we see any evidence of this punishment having been fulfilled upon the church system in the last days?

When I was a kid, big public scandals involving major church figures were unheard of. Back then some Christians felt somewhat self-righteous because the church was considered better than the world. The church generally had a reputation of being holy and church leaders were given special reverence, even by unbelievers. That attitude seems like ancient history today. From about the 1970s forward, there has been an intensifying of exposures of churches and notable church leaders involved in public scandals. This is evidence of the judgments of Revelation chapters 1-3 fulfilled upon the church system in this generation.

EXAMINE THE EVIDENCE OF MESSIAH'S JUDGMENT

It is important for you to understand that this phenomenon is a real fulfillment of Scriptural prophecy. The only way to make that point is to examine the evidence. If we really know Messiah, we should understand that nothing happens by accident. He is in control of all that happens in the midst of the assemblies that profess to represent His Name, meaning that He is ultimately behind public exposures of the clergy. That's what makes the myriad of public exposures of the last 40 years so significant. As unpleasant as this is, we must here review the evidence. The words here following are not my words but are quotes from public sources. Please take the time to read these carefully, because they clearly show that exposures of sins in the church system have been common only in the last 40 years, building up exponentially within that time.

4,392 ACCUSATIONS OF ABUSE ENGULF CATHOLIC CLERGY

"Clerical sexual deviancy allegations have been made against a variety of religious groups including but not exclusively Roman Catholic priests, monks, and nuns...Some incidents involved diocesan priests and members of the various Roman Catholic religious orders, with reports coming from the United States and Ireland. Cases

involved seminaries, schools, orphanages and other institutions (such as the Irish industrial schools) where children were in the care of clergy. Criticism of the Church and its leadership focused on the failure to act upon information, and often to move priests who had received complaints from church to church in order to protect them. Some allegations have led to successful prosecutions of the accused, as well as civil cases settling for millions of dollars...The John Jay Report, commissioned by the U.S. Conference of Catholic Bishops, found accusations against 4,392 priests in the USA, equaling about 4% of all U.S. Priests." (http:/en.wikipedia.org/wiki/Roman_Catholic_sex_abuse_cases)

2008—POPE STATES HE IS SHAMED BY SEXUAL ABUSE SCANDALS

"WASHINGTON (CNN) April 16, 2008—Pope Benedict XVI on Wednesday addressed...the sex abuse scandal in the Roman Catholic Church... He spoke at a prayer service with U.S. bishops at Washington's Basilica of the National Shrine of the Immaculate Conception, the largest Roman Catholic church in North America. Benedict said the sexual abuse of children by priests has caused a "deep shame" and called it "gravely immoral behavior."

"Many of you have spoken to me of the enormous pain that your communities have suffered when clerics have betrayed...their obligations," he told the bishops. Responding to the situation has not been easy and was sometimes very badly handled, the Pope admitted."

1,676 REPORTS OF ABUSE BY DENOMINATIONAL LEADERS

At the time of this writing the *reformation.com* website contains 1,676 distinct news reports of non-Catholic ministers from all Protestant denominations accused of sexually abusing children!

HIGH PROFILE EVANGELICAL SCANDALS

"A series of scandals resulted in the harming of the reputations of several famous American Christian evangelists...This list only includes high-profile evangelist scandals." (Roman Catholic clergy and high-profile leaders from New Religious Movements are not within the scope of this list. http://en.wikipedia.org/wiki/Christian_evangelist_scandals)

LIST OF CHRISTIAN EVANGELISTS
[INVOLVED IN HIGH PROFILE SCANDALS]

1.1 Aimee Semple McPherson, 1920s-40s
1.2 Lonnie Frisbee, 1970s - 1980s
1.3 Oral Roberts, 1977 and 1986
1.4 Jim & Tammy Bakker and Jimmy Swaggart, 1986 and 1991
1.5 Peter Popoff, 1987
1.6 Mike Warnke, 1991
1.7 Robert Tilton, 1991
1.8 Frank Houston, 2000
1.9 John Paulk, 2000
1.10 Douglas Goodman, 2004
1.11 Kent Hovind, 2006
1.12 Ted Haggard, 2006
1.13 Paul Barnes, 2006
1.14 Richard Roberts, 2007
1.15 Bishop Thomas Wesley Weeks and Juanita Bynum, 2007
1.16 Bishop Earl Paulk, 2007
1.17 Phil Driscoll, 2007

SCANDAL OVERTURNS LEADER OF 30,000,000 USA EVANGELICALS

"TED HAGGARD, was leader of the National Association of Evangelicals (NAE) from 2003 until November 2006...The National Association of Evangelicals (NAE) is an agency dedicated to coordinating cooperative ministry for evangelical denominations of Protestant Christians in the United States...There are currently 60 denominations with about 45,000 churches in the organization.

In 2005, Haggard was listed by Time magazine as one of the top 25 most influential evangelicals in America. Haggard is a firm supporter of President George W. Bush, and is sometimes credited with rallying evangelicals behind Bush during the 2004 election. Author Jeff Sharlet reported in 2005 that Haggard "talks to... Bush or his advisers every Monday" and stated at that time that "no pastor in America holds more sway over the political direction of evangelicalism." In a June 2005 Wall Street Journal article, "Ted Haggard, the head of the 30-million strong National Association of Evangelicals, joked that the only disagreement between himself and the leader of the Western world is automotive: Mr. Bush drives a Ford pickup, whereas he prefers a Chevy."

On November 1, 2006, Mike Jones [a male prostitute] stated that Haggard ... had paid [him for services] on an almost monthly basis over the previous three years. Jones contends the relationship was strictly physical, not emotional, and that he was typically paid a "couple of hundred dollars" but sometimes Haggard would pay him extra. Jones also stated "[Haggard] had told me he loved snorting meth..."

On November 3, 2006, Haggard resigned his leadership of the National Association of Evangelicals. The National Association of Evangelicals posted a statement accepting his resignation. Leith Anderson was appointed as the new president on November 7, 2006.

The "Overseer Board of New Life Church" released a prepared statement on the afternoon of November 4, 2006 that stated: "Our investigation and Pastor Haggard's public statements have proven without a doubt that he has committed sexually immoral conduct." The board cited the bylaws of the megachurch and said his conduct compelled them to remove him from his job."

In August 2007, Haggard released a statement asking for monetary donations to help support his family while he and his wife attend classes at the University of Phoenix, a university offering online degrees. The former pastor also said that his family was moving into the Dream Center, a Phoenix based halfway house which ministers to recovering convicts, drug addicts, prostitutes etc. Haggard is pursuing a degree in counseling while his wife Gayle is studying psychology.

News media pointed to his reported income: in 2006, he received $115,000 for the 10 months he worked and also received an $85,000 anniversary bonus shortly before the scandal broke; after the scandal broke, the board of trustees of New Life Church agreed to give him a $138,000 severance. Additionally, the Haggards have a home in Colorado Springs, Colorado that is valued at more than $700,000 and Haggard still receives royalties from books he has authored. (Quotes in this section are from: http://en.wikipedia.org/wiki/Ted_Haggard and http://en.wikipedia.org/wiki/National_Association_of_Evangelicals)

LET'S SUMMARIZE THE EVIDENCE

The number of all these public scandals taken together is staggering, with child sexual abuse accusations against 4,392 Catholic priests uncovered in the USA, and at least 1,676 news items online alleging sexual abuse of children by clergy of all other denominations. That's **over 6,000 alleged cases by clergy of all denominations** having been exposed **in the USA** alone! These figures include only exposures of one sort of sin and do not take into account exposures of all other sins of clergy. It is no wonder the Pope himself felt constrained in 2008 to offer apologies for these sins of the discredited clergy!

Then we have the list of high profile evangelical scandals. This particular list applies to the evangelical Christian world. There are 17 high profile cases listed. One dates back to the 1920s. That's the only case on the list before the 1970s. That gap represents a period of about 50 years in which there were no other such cases of scandal reported. Public exposure of sin by major leaders was practically nonexistent before the 1970s. However, **since the 1970s, there have been 16 cases of big name evangelical leaders publicly exposed in the press.** The rate of exposures has picked up dramatically in just the last couple of years. Out of the list of 16 big name evangelists being exposed since the 1970s, we have 3 of them exposed in 2006 alone, and then 4 more exposed in 2007. Out of a list of 16 cases since 1970, we've got 7 cases, almost half, having occurred in just the last two years reported on. Clearly, the rate of high profile exposures of evangelical clergy has increased dramatically recently.

The increase was not only in number of cases, but also in level of importance. **Ted Haggard, as the leader of the NAE,** was as high profile as you could find in the evangelical world, being at the top of that pyramid of 30 million evangelical Christians in America. He was influential, not only religiously, but also politically, reportedly having telephone time with the President every week. That is, until he was removed from his leadership position after being publicly accused in the press as an alleged homosexual and drug abuser. That scandal was so devastating to the stock of Christian conservatives in America that it may have been a contributing factor to the Democratic sweep in the 2008 elections.

The fact that such a **scandal involving the leader of 30 million American evangelicals** could occur, and that it could go on for an extended period of time with nobody discerning it, screams of spiritual blindness. That evangelicals claim they're "born again" and "have the Holy Spirit" yet leaders close to the top claim to have known nothing of this, is an exposure in itself. (Mat 15:14)

THE NEWS REPORTS FURNISH THE EVIDENCE

I'm not judging any of these individuals. That's not my job. I only know what I have seen and read in the news regarding these cases. I'm commenting on the same news available to everybody. That news itself, taken in the aggregate, is evidence that something unprecedented has been going on in the last 40 years. That trend has reached a zenith in just the last few years. There will likely continue to be more exposures of church leaders. However, it is hard to imagine how such exposures could do much more harm to the reputation of the church system than has already been done. At this point in time public opinion regarding organized Christianity has fallen to an all time low. (Joh 5:22, Rom 2:24)

JUDGMENT FOCUSED ON LEADERS OF THE CHURCH SYSTEM

The wholesale judgment against sin within the churches, as prefigured by the seven churches of Revelation, has been especially focused towards the leaders of the church system from the 1970s forward. When we consider Messiah walking among the seven churches judging them, we find Him telling the leaders that they are the ones being held accountable. This same focus on the leaders is exactly what's been happening here. This fulfills the prophetic pattern. (Jer 23:1-2, Eze 34:1-16, Mat 24:45-51)

Realize that all these thousands of fallen church leaders claimed to be ministers of "Jesus Christ." They claimed to be under His protection and ministering by His authority. Yet, their "ministries" have been ruined or greatly hampered by public disgrace. That could not happen on this huge scale except by judgment of Messiah. If we were citing an isolated incident, then a reader would be justified to say, "That really is a horrible thing but I'm not sure if it's a fulfillment of Bible prophecy." However, the timing, scope, and magnitude of these thousands of exposures mark the 40-year period in which they have occurred as a time of judgment of the church system, in which Messiah has been doing exactly what He said. Surely, if this is not a case of Messiah *warring with the long sword out of His mouth* in the midst of the churches, then what would be? The church system today stands nakedly revealed as the last-days anti-type of the rejected seven churches of Revelation. (Rev 3:16-17, 16:15)

WHY YOU HAVE NEVER HEARD THIS BEFORE

Now, here I am pointing out a modern day fulfillment of Scripture. Why do you think you've never heard about this fulfillment of Scripture before?

Could it be because you've been told the seven churches represent "seven historical periods of the church age" which have little to do with events today? Why do you think church leaders would rather say that those seven churches represent seven ages mostly in the past, rather than admit they are a type of this reality we are speaking of here? They don't want to own this. They don't want to own the fact that this massive exposure of gross sin among church leaders is evidence that the church system has been judged and found wanting by Messiah. (Rev 3:18-19, Dan 5:26-27)

AN ATTACK OF THE ENEMY?

Here some might say: "This mass exposure has been a spiritual attack from the enemy, this is not a judgment from Messiah." We could say that's true if the allegations were false. However, there are thousands of exposures of Christian leaders from across the denominational spectrum and in the vast majority of cases the sins exposed have been admitted or proven to be true, many in a court of law. (1Pe 2:16, 3:12, 17)

You can't call that merely an attack of the enemy. That is corruption being judged. That is Messiah *warring* against sin *with the long sword out of His mouth*. He has been warring upon them, exposing their evil deeds, as if to say "They don't represent Me!" How could you get any other message from these facts? (2Pe 2:1-2)

PLEASE DON'T KILL THE MESSENGER!

Pointing out the obvious here will likely make me the subject of attack, including assassination of my character. I expect that from those who are desperate to protect the church system and their privileged place in it. To those folks I would say, you can kill the messenger but it will do you little good, since the church system is already discredited by the widely-known evil deeds of thousands of your church leaders. This remains true regardless of whatever you may do to me.

EVIDENCE THAT DEMANDS A VERDICT

To all sincere believers I say, look at this message and compare it to reality. Compare what you have actually seen in the news yourself. You be the judge. Is this message true or not? Clearly, I'm telling you the truth as proven out by documented, observable facts–real events. Actually, this should be an encouragement to us all because, as we see Bible prophecy fulfilled, it only confirms to us that the end of the age has arrived. His return is getting closer. However, I'm here to tell you that the unfolding of the end-time picture is going to work out much differently than most of us have been led to believe. This Revelation study paints a vastly different picture of end-time events than you have ever heard before. It is different because it is based on the truth, while much of what you have been taught by the church system is dangerously in error, having been devised mostly to prop up a dying religious system as long as possible. Be fooled no longer! (Mat 7:13-23, 2Ti 3:1-5)

JUDGMENT HAS STARTED WITH THE HOUSE OF GOD

Let's return to the main point here. Judgment must start with the House of God. That's what this is all about. This final generation is an age of judgment. When this final generation began, the first order of business was judgment of the House of God according to the Scriptural principle that judgment must start with the House of God. This is why this judgment of the church system has been going on for 40 years. This is evidence that the Book of Revelation has in fact begun and is now well into its last days fulfillment in this final generation. Messiah has been moving in the midst of the menorahs as the Scriptures show, inspecting the churches with eyes like a fiery flame, judging each one according to their deeds—just as it says in the Book of Revelation. We see in the news that He has been exposing the sins of the church system to the world. His purpose in the judgment is to identify the overcomers whom He will thereafter use to manifest the light of His menorah to the world in the time yet remaining before His Return. How long must this judgment period last?

40 YEARS OF JUDGMENT

Scripturally, the period of judgment of the House of God is 40 years. There are at least 15 judgment periods identified in Scripture, all of them 40 years in length. Some of these are trials and judgment through times of adversity and others are trials and judgment through abundance, such as with the church of Laodicea in Revelation. We find both sorts of judgments in Revelation chapters 1-3.

These 40-year judgment periods include Moses in Egypt, Moses in Midian, and Israel in the wilderness. Later in Israelite history, a number of the judges and leaders of Israel presided over 40-year periods of judgment, including Judge Othniel, High Priest Eli, Judge Barak, and Judge Gideon. Philistine oppression was allowed for 40 years to test and judge the people of Israel. The people were tested and judged for 40 years under King Saul. The people came through a favorable 40-year judgment during the reign of David, and following that, under the reign of Solomon. Forty-year judgment periods also occurred with the reigns of Jeroboam II, King Jehoash, King Joash, and then, of course, from the start of Messiah's ministry about 30 A.D. until the destruction of the temple in 70 A.D. All of these precedents establish beyond doubt that the period of judgment of the House of God must be 40 years. This 40-year judgment period is so firmly fixed in Scripture that it must also apply to Messiah's inspection and judgment in the midst of the churches in these last days. (Act 7:23,30, 13:21, Deu 8:2-5, Psa 95:10, Jdg 3:11, 1Sa 4:18, Jdg 5:31, 8:28,13:1, 2Sa 5:2,4, 1Ki 11:42, 2Ki 12:1-3, 12-14, 2Ch 24:1, Mat 12:39)

ISRAEL'S 40 YEARS OF JUDGMENT IN THE WILDERNESS

Now, let's learn more by considering Israel's 40-year judgment in the wilderness. At the close of that 40-year period, Moses spoke to the new generation and reminded them what had happened over those 40 years. He said:

> You shall observe to do all the commandments which I command you this day, that you may live, and multiply, and go in and possess the land which YHWH swore to your fathers. You shall

> remember all the way which YHWH your God has led you these forty years in the wilderness, that He might humble you, to prove you, to know what was in your heart, whether you would keep His commandments, or not. (Deu 8:1-2)

Moses reminds the new generation why that first generation that came out of Egypt had been subjected to 40 years of testing. That they might be humbled, that they might be proved and that YHWH might know what was in their hearts. In the judgment, they would prove whether or not they would keep His commandments, whether they would obey Him, and be true to Him. This is what testing and judgment is all about.

JUDGMENT ALLOWS TIME FOR CORRECTION AND REPENTANCE

In the Greco-Roman mindset, people think of judgment as something that happens very quickly as the end of a process. For example, if you live a life of crime, one day you go into the courtroom, you go through your trial, and you get sentenced. That sentence is thought to be your judgment. The 40-year judgment in the wilderness demonstrates that for YHWH judgment is not the end of the process only. Judgment is not just punishment. Judgment is a time of testing to prove the hearts of persons, even to give them a chance to be humbled, and a chance to repent and turn around and change their lives. This is an evidence of God's goodness, His kindness towards His children. He doesn't want to bring punishment until He first allows ample time of judgment in which the righteous are corrected and proved, that they may turn around and choose the good way. Forty years of judgment is a liberal amount of time to be corrected. Sin persisting through that lengthy period cannot be blamed on lack of maturity or ignorance because 40 years is more than enough time to grow and change and discover deceptions and correct them–if anyone has a heart to do so.

THE JUDGMENT OF YHWH IS GOOD!

In all of this we see the good heart of YHWH towards His own in judging them 40 years in the wilderness. He instructed them as sons:

> He humbled you, and allowed you to be hungry, and fed you with manna, which you didn't know, neither did your fathers know; that He might make you know that man does not live by bread only, but man lives by everything that proceeds out of the mouth of YHWH. You shall consider in your heart that as a man chastens his son, so YHWH your God chastens you." (Deu 8:3, 5)

Do you understand what this is saying? YHWH's object was not to cause His people to all die as sinners in the wilderness. He wasn't eager to punish them. Rather, He humbled them because they needed to be humbled. They thought more highly of themselves than their behavior merited. They needed to repent. In order to repent, one needs to be humble. He allowed them to be hungry and then He fed them with manna. In this He showed them that they needed to trust in Him. They needed to live by every word out of His mouth. He wanted them to see that He is a good Father, that they might be blessed. He chastens His people. Those who will accept it, those who will be chastened by Him and will be changed and will be humbled and will repent, they're the ones that get the blessing.

OVERCOMERS SEIZED THE PROMISE!

It's so sad that only two people of that generation entered into the Promised Land, those being Joshua and Caleb. They were the remnant of that generation, two people that entered into the Promised Land leading the younger generation in with them to receive the blessing. All the rest died in the wilderness, never rising up to their full potential in righteousness. This is what came out of those 40 years of judgment of Israel in the wilderness.

ISRAEL IMMERSED INTO MESSIAH AT THE RED SEA

This 40 years of testing of Israel is prophetic of the testing of the believers in Messiah at the end of the age. We see this from something that Paul the apostle said to the Corinthians in 1 Corinthians chapter 10. Let's read a few passages that prove the point.

> Now I would not have you ignorant, brothers, that our fathers were all under the cloud, and all passed through the sea; and were all immersed into Moses in the cloud and in the sea; and all ate the same spiritual food; and all drank the same spiritual drink. For they drank of a spiritual rock that followed them, and the rock was Messiah. (1Co 10:1-4)

Paul speaks of the experience of Israel being delivered at the Red Sea from the Egyptians. It was as if Israel was immersed at that time, because their life was all but lost and yet they passed through the sea, underneath the cloud through the parted waters. In this amazing immersion, they were given new life. Their Rock was Messiah. These were the favored ones. Their Egyptian enemies were not favored, but were all washed away in the waters in a dramatic display of Divine deliverance.

Recently, I was reading the song Israel sang after the Red Sea crossing. It was a triumphant song lifting up what YHWH had done. The song speaks of the favor that they had enjoyed. It speaks of the fear the Red Sea miracle put into the Canaanites in the Promised Land, preparing the way for Israel to enter and take the Promised Land. The Red Sea deliverance was an extremely triumphant time for Israel there at the beginning. It was an event pregnant with promise for that favored generation of Israel. For that reason Paul's next verse is so poignantly shocking and tragic.

THE TRAGIC OUTCOME FOR THE WILDERNESS GENERATION

> However with most of them, God was not well pleased, for they were overthrown in the wilderness. (1Co 10:5)

That's a sour note. God was not well pleased with most of them because they did not live up to their potential. They sang about going into the Promised Land but when it came time to actually do it, what happened? Fear and unbelief overcame them. They became crippled by unbelief and disobedience. Most of them were overthrown in the wilderness, which is to say, they died in the wilderness. Amazing, considering what they had seen at the Red Sea.

CHEAP GRACE DOESN'T CUT IT!

Here some might say, "Yes, that's what happened to Israel, but that can't happen to Christians because Christians are under grace." If you are inclined to take that attitude you need to read the very next verse.

> Now these things were our examples, to the intent we should not lust after evil things, as they also lusted. (1Co 10:6)

40 YEARS WILDERNESS JUDGMENT-OUR EXAMPLE

What? These things that happened to Israel *were our examples*? That is, for believers of Messiah? That is what Paul said. That means the majority of believers could be overthrown just like the Israelites were. Why should believers today think that they're going to be treated differently than God's nation in the past? This is a big lie. God does not change.

Let's read on:

> Now these things were our examples, to the intent we should not lust after evil things, as they also lusted. Neither be idolaters, as some of them were. As it is written, "The people sat down to eat and drink, and rose up to play." Neither let us commit sexual immorality, as some of them committed, and in one day twenty-three thousand fell. Neither let us test the Lord, as some of them tested, and perished by the serpents. Neither grumble, as some of them also grumbled, and perished by the destroyer. Now all these things happened to them by way of example, and they were written for our admonition, on whom the ends of the ages have come. Therefore let him who thinks he stands be careful that he doesn't fall. (1Co 10:6-12)

PAUL'S MESSAGE DOESN'T SOUND "CHRISTIAN"

This is a very different sort of message than you're likely to hear in Christian churches today. Paul does <u>not</u> say, "No worries mate, the Old Testament is now done away"—quite the opposite. Paul is unmistakably telling 'saved believers' in Messiah that the 40 years of trial in the wilderness, in which Israelites were falling by the thousands left and right, was "*written for our admonition on whom the ends of the ages have come.*" Then he says, "*Therefore let him who thinks he stands be careful that he does not fall.*"

When you consider what happened with the Israelites during their 40 years of judgment, in which they were falling to sin by the thousands, then you look at the thousands of news reports exposing the sins of church leaders over the last 40 years–does it ring a bell? It's the same thing and the same word to the wise: *Let him who thinks he stands be careful that he does not fall.* Believers in Messiah can fall. That is the message here.

A MESSAGE FOR THE ENDS OF THE AGES

Paul's words are very precise in citing the 40-year wilderness judgment of Israel, saying these things are examples *for our admonition on whom the ends of the ages have come.* "*Ends*" is a plural word so has an "s" on the end. "*Ages*" is a plural word also. The phrase is translated correctly here as *ends of the ages.* What does this unusual phrase mean?

Paul's words indicate he was thinking of his own generation at the end of that age in which he was living. Paul wrote these words near the end of the 40 years of judgment upon Israel that ended in 70 A.D. However, since he speaks of plural ends of ages it is clear he had a second end of an age also in mind. Paul is suggesting a double fulfillment upon generations of two different ages, each living at the end of their respective age. The second end of the age embraced within Paul's plural phrase could be none other than the end of the age when Messiah will return.

THE END OF THE AGE STARTED IN 1967

Messiah had indicated that second end of the age would commence at the end of the *times of the Gentiles.* Y'shua indicated that Jerusalem would be the time clock. So long as Jerusalem remained in Gentile hands the *times of the Gentiles* would dominate. However, when Jerusalem finally would come back under Israelite rule, the *times of the Gentiles* would be over. That change would mark the beginning of the final generation at the end of the age. For nearly 1900 years Jerusalem was the world's football, experiencing *times* under various Gentile powers until, in 1967, Israel took back control of Jerusalem in the Six-Day War. This event marked the end of the *times of the Gentiles* and began the end of the age in which we now live. Messiah promises that this final generation *shall not pass away* until all is fulfilled and Messiah returns. Count on it. (Luk 21:24-33)

PAUL'S THREE 40-YEAR PARALLEL JUDGMENT PERIODS

Now, back to Paul; he was writing about the 40-year period of judgment of Israel in the wilderness, saying it was an example for believers during plural *ends of the ages*. He was writing near the end of the 40-year period of judgment which ended with the destruction of Jerusalem in 70 A.D. That was the end of the age he was living in. His words indicate yet another end of the age in which there would be a 40-year judgment, which is the end of the age in which we have been living since 1967.

THE 40-YEAR JUDGMENT PERIOD OF THE CHURCH SYSTEM

Now, putting these facts together with the Scriptural principle that judgment must start with the House of God we must conclude that the judgment of the churches began in 1967. According to Scriptural precedent and Paul's prophetic words this judgment period must last 40 years. **The 40 years were up in the year of 2007.** That timing matches the data from the news we have already considered. From 1967, at the beginning of the judgment period, a few years were allowed for the first offenders to repent before any exposure occurred. Then, in the 1970s, these judgments, including exposures of evil in the highest leadership of the church system began, growing in intensity through the 40-year period of judgment. As would be expected, these exposures were greatly intensified towards the end of the 40-year judgment period. We have documented the prophetic pattern and we have documented the literal fulfillment, which we have all observed. There is also much more supporting material, including the many prophetic references to a great apostasy in these last days. This will be discussed in more detail later in our study. I only mention it here to say this: We've been seeing bad fruit of that great apostasy being exposed through these last 40 years. All of this has been fulfilling Bible prophecy. So where does that put us now?

WHERE IS THE PUNISHMENT?

Let's revisit the actual seven churches of Asia for an indication. As we have seen, they are a type of the entire church system of the final generation professing "Christ." We saw that punishment did not come immediately on those seven churches of Asia. However, it did come. We saw very dramatically that their menorah was literally removed from its place—their witness was completely removed. That fulfillment of Messiah's warning was extremely dramatic.

In the same pattern, the church system of this generation has been inspected and found wanting. The judgment is concluded and over with the year of 2007 (1967+40=2007 inclusive). That entire system has been judged as unfit to represent Messiah. Their menorah has been removed. Now, I'm not saying that is the case with all individuals. I am talking about the entire church system itself. I have presented ample evidence that the entire multidenominational church system has been inspected and has been rejected. Revelation indicates final punishment will fall upon that doomed system in its then mutated form, later, in the Great Tribulation.

NOW THE TRIBULATION WILL START, RIGHT?...NOT!

At this point some may be thinking: "OK, the 40-year judgment of the church system is concluded. Cool! It's just seven more years to glory!"

Not so fast! There is more yet slated on the prophetic time-table before we get to the last segment of the "game." Realize that the end result of the lengthy period of judgment of the church system was to identify and set apart a company of overcomers to carry the ball for the Kingdom through the remainder of the "game." Problem is, the Overcomers haven't even figured out they need to be a team yet! There is still a lot of work to be done before the Overcomers take to the field in one accord, let alone actually go on to win the prize. Don't worry. Though the clock is ticking down toward the finish, there is still time!

In this new phase, everyone will have their hearts tried through the trials coming upon the world system. The judgment of the world system now emerging will produce a complex snarl of troubles, which will intensify in successive waves toward an ultimate climax, for what we all will feel is much too long a time. The purpose of that time of trial, once again, is to identify and separate out the righteous from the wicked, that they may be delivered for a purpose, that YHWH may be glorified in them. (Gen 18:23-25, Exo 23:7, Psa 7:9, Mal 3:18)

We're not there yet. We're not at the place where the company of overcomers has been identified and been drawn together as a unified whole. The world does not yet see them united, lifting up that menorah in the Name of Messiah, in such a way that the whole world can see their Light as a place of safety to run to. There is a period of time allowed for that to occur in the prophetic time-table. Since that is true, we can't possibly be at the beginning of the Great Tribulation period right now. It's premature.

I'm sorry to have to say that, because all of the overcomers long for the Return of Messiah and we want that to happen as soon as possible. However, I dare not say what you want to hear just to sell books. Not only would my Master rightly chastise me, but far too much is at stake for you. What happens if you expend all you've got on the next seven years and then the finish line remains out of sight? Better you know that this is an endurance race and not a sprint. That's what you need to know to win the prize. With all my heart, I want you to win the prize! (Gal 1:10, 1Co 13:2, 2Co 9:24, 11:2-3, Luk 14:27-35)

ADOPT THE OVERCOMER MINDSET!

As we go on in this study of the Book of Revelation, you will come to understand that there is a plan and a program now under way in which all must be fulfilled. You will find that until now most of that prophetic program has been passed over by all interpreters of Revelation. In fact, the most important aspects of the prophetic picture have been entirely ignored until now. This is why we must do a careful investigation of the Book of Revelation point upon point, upon point, led by the Spirit, so that we can fully enter in to what YHWH is doing right now.

This is the end of the age. This is the generation in which everything must be settled up. YHWH is going to dot every "i" and cross every "t" before we get to the very end. That is why there is still time as of this writing before the Great Tribulation will begin. That remaining time must not be wasted or frittered away.

The remainder of this book will explain why you are now, and will be, seeing grave consequences of sin coming upon the world. If you are lax, if you are double-minded, if you are not in vital relationship with Messiah and walking in Him, then the same judgments that fall upon the world will fall upon you–perhaps some have already. You can't afford to let that keep happening because you have a higher calling than that. If you are mired down in useless muck with the world because you were too spiritually lazy to discern and walk in His path, then what use will you be to His plan?

This is not a time to be spiritually lax, though it is reason to take a longer view—to realize Messiah told us that we must *endure to the end.* We must persevere. ***The one that endures to the end will be saved.*** We need to get in that mindset, that we will not be deterred by any trial. We will endure in faith. We're going for it. We're digging in, we're converging in unity, and then we're pushing onward together, prevailing past the very gates of Hell, to seize the prize! (1Pe 4:1-5, Jam 4:8-10, 1Jo 2:15-17, Mat 24:13, 16:18, Phl 3:12-15, Heb 12:1-2)

HEAVENLY JUDGMENT COURT

VISITING HEAVEN'S COURTROOM

The Judgment Court Revealed

How does one enter heaven? By invitation only! Notice how Yochanan received his invitation.

> After these things I looked and saw a door opened in heaven, and the first voice that I heard, like a shofar speaking with me, was one saying, "Come up here, and I will show you the things which must happen after this." Immediately I was in the Spirit.
>
> Behold, **there was a Throne set in heaven**, and **One sat on the Throne** that looked like a jasper stone and a sardius. There was a rainbow around the Throne, like an emerald to look at.
>
> **Around the throne** were twenty-four thrones. On the thrones were twenty-four elders sitting, dressed in white garments, with crowns of gold on their heads. **Out of the Throne** proceeded lightnings and thunders and sounds.
>
> There were seven lamps of fire burning **before His Throne**, which are the Seven Spirits of God. **Before the Throne** was something like a sea of glass, similar to crystal. (Rev 4:1-6a. Emphasis added. Text refined as explained throughout this chapter. Compare with KJV.)

WHAT ARE WE LOOKING AT?

When you enter a room for the first time you can discern a lot simply by looking around. The calendar on the wall gives you a time context, perhaps having some special events marked on it. Usually, at a minimum, you can tell what the room is used for, and by that, what goes on there. If there are people in the room, where they sit, how they are dressed, and what they do all help to fill out the picture. Your personal scan of the room helps you get a sense of what to expect during your presence there. This sort of meaningful big picture of the Heavenly Judgment Court has been lacking up until now.

Here is what you are seeing upon entering the Heavenly Court:

THE CALENDAR

The first verse gives us timing indications, much like a calendar on the wall. Yochanan starts chapter four by saying: *After these things I looked.* When he says, *after these things,* what things must he be talking about? Logically, as he starts chapter 4 he means *after* chapters 1-3 of Revelation had been concluded. Only then did Yochanan see *a door open in heaven.* On seeing the door, he heard *a voice like a shofar.* Shofars are meant to be alarming, so this voice certainly got his attention. Shofars signal important scheduled events, indicating he was being summoned to a very important scheduled event. The voice said, *Come up here and I will show you what must occur after these things.*

In going through the door Yochanan was not only entering heaven–he was entering heaven <u>in the future from his day</u>... seeing *what must occur after these things.* He was entering heaven *after* the fulfillment of Revelation 1-3, which fulfillment we have already disclosed as ending with 2007, inclusive. Since the Biblical year begins in the first spring month, the Biblical year which started in 2007 ended in springtime of 2008. What Yochanan saw in heaven began in the spring of 2008, in the first month of the new Biblical year, immediately after the 40-year judgment of the church system had concluded. Yochanan immediately found himself through the door in that place and time, *in the Spirit.*

THE THRONE WAS SET

On entering heaven, the first thing Yochanan saw was the Throne being *set.* All other furnishings, persons, and actions are thereafter spoken of in relation to the Throne. *On the Throne, around the Throne, out of the Throne, before His Throne, in the midst of the Throne,* are the references positioning all else there. Clearly, the *Throne set in heaven* is the focal point of this heavenly scene.

Most commentators see this as the Throne in the Sanctuary of YHWH in heaven. Their doctrine is inconsistent with a movable Throne. Therefore, a number of translations of Scripture read as if the Throne is stationary and YHWH is found sitting upon it from the start. For example, the NIV renders the verse: *there before me was a throne in heaven with someone sitting on it.* (Rev 4:2b NIV)

Religious sensibilities not withstanding, that rendering of the NIV and similar popular versions is not correct. Here is that same verse literally parsed according to *Strong's* numbering system.

> behold[2400] [5628], a throne[2362] was set[2749] [5711] in[1722] heaven[3772] and[2532] one sat[2521] [5740] on[1909] the throne[2362].

The literal sense of this verse is unmistakable. Yochanan looked on as a Throne was set in place and One sat down upon it. The Throne is being set in place just as the scene opens. In fact, the Throne was set in place on a large, raised platform, though the platform is not specifically mentioned at this point. The platform raises the Throne high above all other furnishings in view. Once the Throne was set in place, the entire Throne area dominated by the Divine Presence, including the platform, is called *the Throne.* In this way YHWH was seated high up, in a commanding position above everyone else. All this signifies that Yochanan arrived just in time for the start of a special kind of meeting in heaven to occur in a different part of heaven than where YHWH is usually found to dwell. The Throne was set in this place and then YHWH sat upon it, bringing the meeting to order, just as when a judge takes his seat in a courtroom today. (Compare Isa 6:1-3, Dan 7:9-10)

THE PORCH OF JUDGMENT

To be more precise, this is exactly what happened when a king of ancient Israel judged his people. He did not judge from his usual throne room. His throne would be set upon an elevated platform in an area especially used for judgment, where he would judge before all onlookers at the appointed time. In fact, Solomon's Palace was built with a *Porch of Judgment* for the very purpose we are discussing here. *[Solomon] made the porch of the throne where he was to judge, even the Porch of Judgment.* Being a porch, the official judgment area was opened up to the outside. This would allow for the public to view the king's judgment of his people. (1Ki 7:7)

Today kings are not thought of as judges. By contrast, in ancient Israel righteous judgment was a fundamental responsibility of the king. When Solomon was asked of YHWH what He should give him, Solomon asked for wisdom to judge the people. YHWH was so pleased with this request that He told Solomon:

> Because this was in your heart, and you have not asked riches, wealth, or honor, nor the life of those who hate you, neither yet have asked long life; but have asked wisdom and knowledge for yourself, **that you may judge my people**, over whom I have made you king: wisdom and knowledge is granted to you. I will give you riches, wealth, and honor, such as none of the kings have had who have been before you; neither shall there any after you have the like. (2Ch 1:11-12)

Multitudes of Israelites came to Solomon's Porch of Judgment to observe and listen to the amazing righteous judgments from the mouth of the king. Similar to court proceedings today, all with an interest in a case assembled before the judgment throne was set and the king took his seat. The king's entrance signaled the start of the judgment proceedings. It is very rude indeed to show up *after* the king is seated and proceedings begin! The government of Israel is patterned after the heavenly Government. This is what we're seeing here in the Book of Revelation. Yochanan entered just before the start of a scheduled judgment meeting of the Supreme King. The Throne was set in place and One sat upon the Throne and that One was YHWH. With YHWH seated upon the Throne, the Divine Court is now in session. The judgment of the world now hangs in the balance, before the Throne. (1Ki 3: 16-28, 2Ch 9:1-8, Psa 72:1, Pro 25:6, 29:14, Luk 11:31)

ONE SAT ON THE THRONE

We're told here that the One who sat on the Throne looked like a *jasper stone* and a *sardius stone*, also known as *carnelian*. Both of these stones are red. These are the first and the last stone in the *Breastplate of Judgment* worn by the High Priest. When the High Priest was to judge the people, he was to wear the Breastplate of Judgment. The fact that *jasper and sardius* are the first and the last stone in that breastplate suggests to us that the Twelve Tribes of Israel are encompassed within these judgment proceedings. The world is to be judged by the God of Israel on Israel's behalf. Also, there is something regarding YHWH and His character reflected in the Twelve Tribes of Israel. There is a similarity, a likeness unto. That was His purpose regarding the Nation of Israel from the start; to reflect His own glory in this world through Israel. (Exo 28:15-30, 29:43, 39:8-21, Lev 11:45, Isa 46:13, 59:15-19)

Jasper and sardius are both the color red, which color actually relates to blood in Hebrew. Though both are red, these two stones are somewhat different in appearance. One of them is variegated in color and the other is a consistent, shining red stone. These speak of blood in its two aspects. On the one hand, blood suggests judgment in its many expressions from mercy to severity. On the other hand, blood represents the great constant love of our Father in giving His Son as a sacrifice for us. Justice and love in perfect balance here describe YHWH as Judge on the Throne. (Exo 20:5-6, Deu 10:17-21, Isa 4:4, Jer 22:3, Eze 23:45, Jam 1:17, Joh 3:16-17, 1Jo 1:5-10, 3:1-10, 16, 4:16-21)

A RAINBOW AROUND THE THRONE LIKE EMERALD

An emerald, of course, is the color green. In the sunshine, it's translucent. It glows. The intensely glowing green Light around the Throne looks like a rainbow in the sense that a rainbow in the sky appears to the eye as if one is observing a flat surface of light. Also, a rainbow has different gradients of color. This emerald rainbow-like Light has those same characteristics. It is not a great orb of Light. Rather, when at rest, it goes around the Throne from one side of the Throne over the top of the Throne and on to the other side of the Throne. It actually continues under the Throne to the starting point, forming what appears like a giant variegated green disk of Light going out from the Throne all the way around. When you're looking straight on, you see the rainbow around the Throne as a huge, flat, glowing disk of intense green Light completely around the Throne, though only the top half, in the half-circle of a rainbow, is in view from above. Though it is a shining emerald green color it has gradients of different shades of green. Like a rainbow, but all shades of green.

Unlike a rainbow, this green Light doesn't only look flat. It actually *is* flat! It is very thin, precise, and intense; more like a laser light than an ordinary light. This may sound strange to you, but a person may be 'scanned' by this Light from the Throne. In other words, this Light can be directed to pass through a person's entire body, slowly, from one side to the other, as a 'sheet' of Light. The 'sheet' of Light doesn't change at all on contact with a person's body. Instead, it holds its own composition and integrity as it passes through. To the subject, it feels as if it is realigning every cell in the subject's body, as if every cell is being 'recalibrated' to the Light of heaven, as it passes through.

This Light is the Divine Life that proceeds from the Throne. This Divine Life is a projection of the very Eternal Life and Character of the One on the Throne. All of the covenants of YHWH are projections from His Throne of His Divine Life in relationship to man. This is why the rainbow was used as a sign of the Covenant with Noah on behalf of all mankind. In a larger sense, the rainbow is the source and symbol of all of the covenants of YHWH. The covenants draw and ultimately lead the righteous home to partake of His Divine Life forever. (Gen 9:13, Psa 36:9, Pro 6:23, 16:15, Isa 8:20, 51:4, Joh 1:4-5, 8:12)

Now that we have an initial grasp of the Throne and its Principle Occupant let us look out from there to view the other furnishings and distinguished persons of the Heavenly Court.

AROUND THE THRONE WERE 24 THRONES

After describing the Throne and the One who sat upon it we would normally expect that Yochanan would next describe the *four living creatures* that were *in the midst of the throne, and around the throne.* This would logically complete the description of the Throne area. That Yochanan did otherwise was a purposeful choice. We will take Yochanan's lead and consider them later also.

In next describing ***the twenty-four thrones*** and the ***twenty-four Elders*** being seated upon them Yochanan gives us the next most important information describing the meeting, and the next thing in view in the scene. Being an Israelite, you can be sure Yochanan's next priority after the Throne concerns Israel. Why? Next to the Throne, the top priority for every true Israelite is Israel. These 24 Elders are thus seen assembling for a vital meeting concerning Israel. (Psa 137:1-6)

Typically, most readers imagine *around the Throne* to literally mean that the 24 thrones are arranged in a full circle with the Throne of YHWH in the center, like the hub of a wheel. This picture misses the true intent of the phrase. Here is another verse with similar wording:

> And he looked round about[2945] on them which[3588] sat[2521] about[4012] him (Mar 3:34a)

Here, a form of the word translated as *around* in Revelation 4:4 is literally translated as *round about* in Mark 3:34a. In this verse Messiah looked out on those who sat around him, that is, in a circle going out from Him on either side of Him. Rather than being positioned in the center like the hub of a wheel the entire group was arranged in a circle going out from Messiah, for the purpose of a meeting.

Perhaps you have gathered for a meeting like this at some point. Prayer and fellowship meetings are often arranged in this fashion today wherein chairs are arranged in a circle, with the group leader at one end of the circle. This allows for everyone to see the leader and each other to participate in the meeting. Council meetings are often arranged like this, as are board meetings. Such meetings are often around a large table with the chairman at one end. Government meetings often operate this way, such as cabinet meetings and the like. Certainly with thrones and crowns, and the governmental number of 24, government is in view in the Heavenly Court.

This is the true picture of the 24 thrones. They are already in the room, raised, but not as high as the Throne of YHWH. They are arranged in two arcs going out and forward from either side of the Throne, with 12 thrones on each side. On one end is the Throne of YHWH and on the other is *something like a sea of glass, similar to crystal.* We will get to that shortly.

ON THE THRONES WERE 24 ELDERS SITTING

> On the thrones were twenty-four elders sitting, dressed in white garments, with crowns of gold on their heads. (Rev 4:4b)

As Yochanan entered and observed the Throne being set, he saw 24 Elders in the act of sitting; that is, taking their seats, on their thrones. They were gathering there for the meeting at the appointed time. This is another indication that the meeting was just about to begin, as Yochanan entered the Heavenly Court.

They are numbered at 24, they are called Elders, they sit on the 24 thrones, they wear white garments, and they wear crowns of gold. That's all we are told here about them. Who are they?

ELDERS OF THE TRIBES OF ISRAEL

The 24 Elders are given no further introduction, as if you should already know who they are. If you, like Yochanan, are a renewed Israelite who grasps the governmental order of YHWH you know.

Elders (G4245 *presbuteros*) literally means *old men.* This word is never used of spirit beings and is always used of men. "Old women" is translated from a different form of the word (G4247 *presbutis*). Unlike our modern world, ancient Israel highly valued the wisdom and experience of advanced years. In ancient Israel, the old men were the fathers of the tribes and clans. This made them the leaders of that patriarchal nation. Thus the word *elder* refers to more than just a man's age; it also denotes an office of authority in the government of Israel that was generally reserved for the mature men of experience and wisdom. Each tribe had many elders with one head elder, a father-ruler (*patriarch*), a chieftain/prince (*nasi*) who represented his tribe at the highest level, having authority over the other levels of elders subordinate to him within his tribe. Each of these tribal heads ruled in the place of his deceased tribal father before him, all the way back to the original sons of Jacob–the ultimate 12 Elders of Israel. When matters arose that concerned the whole nation the then ruling 12 tribal heads would meet to decide a course of action together. (Exo 3:16,4:29, 17:6; 18:12-27, 19:7, Num 1:16, 11:16, 25, 30, Deu 5:23, 21:19-21, 22:18, 27:1, 31:28, 32:7, 33:9, Jos 23-24, 1Sa 8:4, 2Sa 5:1-3, 1Ki 4:7,27, 8:1, 1Ch 23, Psa 107:32, Pro 31:23, Eze 7:26)

The tribal government is strictly based in the family lineage and, as such, springs from natural family authority as established by YHWH from the creation forward. This is the most basic form of government and, in a sense; every Israelite enters into Israel along a path first blazed by one of the 12 Tribal Patriarchs, to belong to a tribe founded by one of them. That is why the gates into the New Jerusalem are ultimately named for the 12 Tribal Patriarchs from whom the tribes sprang. That this is so in the New Jerusalem is proof enough that the tribal government of Israel continues as a vital part of the government of believing Israel today, and will, as long as there is a New Jerusalem. Truly, God does not change, even if the ways of the world do. (Mal 3:6, Rev 21:12)

Thus we see that this tribal form of government persists in Israel at all times as the most basic level of government, continuing even under the kingship. When the tribal heads accepted a king they also accepted the administrative government of a king over the entire nation. This provided a needed balance, because the tribal elders were naturally each concerned mostly with their own tribe, for which they were responsible, rather than for the interests of the nation as a whole. They submitted to David as king precisely for that reason. They came to understand that the nation needed a righteous shepherd with the good of the entire nation at heart. (1Sa 30:26, 2Sa 5:1-4, 1Ki 8:1-3, 12:1-20, 20:7-8, 1Ch 11:1-3, 21:16, 2Ch 5:2)

ELDERS OF THE KINGDOM OF ISRAEL

The king established his own administration separate from, but in concert with, the 12 Elders. Even the kingship is patriarchal in nature, in that, by covenant it belongs to the family of David of the Tribe of Judah. Thus it was natural for the king's family to form the top level of authority of his kingdom administration. Also, the Levites (tribe of Levi) were organized by the king for sacred service, since they were assigned that tribal duty by covenant with YHWH. This is an example of how the kingdom government functioned in concert with the natural tribal government in Israel. On the other hand, the king also chose many leaders irrespective of tribal affiliation, on the basis of character and ability, to serve as elders in the sense of administrators of his kingdom. The kingdom thus opened up opportunity in Israel based, not only on tribal destiny, but based also on personal excellence. (Gen 49:4-10, 2Sa 7:16, Jer 23:20-26, 1Ki 4:1-21, 1Ch 12:1-40, 23:1-29:30, 29:6)

Messiah chose 12 head administrators to eventually rule in His administration over the 12 Tribes of Israel. We usually call them the 12 Apostles. Their role is so critically important to the Kingdom Government that the wall of the New Jerusalem is said to rest on 12 foundations, which are the 12 Apostles. These 12 Apostles are the 12 Elders of the Kingdom administration in that all subsequent spiritual offices in the Kingdom can be said to derive from them, since they are the first appointed witnesses to Messiah. As with the pattern established by David, these do not replace the tribal government of Israel nor do they replace the 12 Elders of the 12 Tribes. The 12 Elders represent the government as issuing from the people up while the Twelve Apostles (12 Kingdom Elders) represent the government as issuing from Messiah down. Both aspects of government are absolutely necessary to perfect government in Yah's plan. (Mat 19:28, Luk 22:28-30, Eph 2:20, Rev 21:14)

THE 24 ELDERS

Thus, 24 Elders on thrones, wearing white garments, wearing crowns of gold, undoubtedly are the glorified 12 sons of Jacob who are the ultimate 12 Elders of the Tribes of Israel joined by the glorified 12 Apostles who are the ultimate 12 Elders of the Messianic Kingdom administration over the 12 Tribes of Israel. Together these 24 Elders are the senior rulers of the entire government of the 12 Tribes of Israel in the great eternal plan of YHWH.

Though the government of Israel absolutely requires the correctness of this teaching some might question it, due to an apparent logical problem. How could Yochanan, being an Apostle himself, be one of the 24 Elders, since that would mean that he is simultaneously shown in the same place twice? Actually, that is only an indication of how scientifically sophisticated Revelation is.

Yochanan of Revelation is an observer who entered into heaven by the Spirit in his own distant future, to observe something that would happen out of time from his natural life, which he was still living. By contrast, the 24 Elders he observed are seen in their future glorified state. This is not only inter-dimensional viewing. It is future viewing as well! Surely, the best way for Yochanan to describe this future scene is to simply say what he saw, without trying to untangle a paradox of the space-time continuum for which there was no language in those days. Today we have something we can relate this to, such as *Back to the Future* and other such stories based on scientific theory that portray exactly the time-travel paradox Yochanan is seen to have experienced in Revelation. Besides, though we know Yochanan was one of the 12 Apostles, nowhere in Revelation does Yochanan ever mention that status, not even when introducing himself, so modest a man was he. How much less then, would he indicate himself to be one of those select 24 Elders in glory! That simply was not his way.

OK, we understand that the 24 Elders are the glorified 24 Elders of the 12 Tribes of Israel. Why then are they assembling in this manner for *this* meeting? There can be only one answer! This is a governmental meeting of the highest level involving matters concerning the 12 Tribes of Israel!

LIGHTNINGS AND THUNDERS AND SOUNDS

Out of the Throne proceeded lightnings and thunders and sounds. This phrase describes the response from the Throne to the gathering of the 24 Elders of Israel at the start of the meeting. YHWH is assuring them in the most concrete terms that the Covenant He made with Israel at Sinai, the Mosaic Covenant, has now come up before the Heavenly Court! Indeed, this is why the 24 Elders of all Israel are gathered there.

Lightnings and thunders and sounds were the physical signs of the Presence of YHWH in cutting the Covenant with the sons of Israel at Sinai, his Divine Signature on the Covenant, if you will. Note the historic record of that event.

> It happened on the third day, when it was morning, that there were thunders and lightnings, and a thick cloud on the mountain, and the sound of an exceedingly loud shofar; and all the people who

> were in the camp trembled. Moses led the people out of the camp to meet God; and they stood at the lower part of the mountain. Mount Sinai, all of it, smoked, because YHWH descended on it in fire; and its smoke ascended like the smoke of a furnace, and the whole mountain quaked greatly. (Exo 19:16-18)

On that day YHWH declared His Commandments to Israel, comprising their side of the Mosaic Covenant. The people were greatly frightened by the manifestation of YHWH.

> All the people perceived the thunderings, the lightnings, the sound of the shofar, and the mountain smoking. When the people saw it, they trembled, and stayed at a distance. They said to Moses, "Speak with us yourself, and we will listen; but don't let God speak with us, lest we die." Moses said to the people, "Don't be afraid, for God has come to test you, and that His fear may be before you, that you won't sin." (Exo 20:18-20)
>
> After YHWH declared all of the Commandments of His Covenant Moses came and told the people all the words of YHWH, and all the ordinances; and all the people answered with one voice, and said, "All the words which YHWH has spoken will we do." (Exo 24:3)

The forefathers entered into the Covenant that day by agreeing to perform all of it. According to the family order of Israel the obligation of the fathers is binding upon the children of all generations of Israel thereafter.

YHWH BOUND HIMSELF TO THE MOSAIC COVENANT

Many don't realize that YHWH declared His obligations under the Covenant of Sinai to Moses first.

> Moses went up to God, and YHWH called to him out of the mountain, saying, "This is what you shall tell the house of Jacob, and tell the sons of Israel: 'You have seen what I did to the Egyptians, and how I bore you on eagles' wings, and brought you to Myself. Now therefore, if you will indeed obey My voice, and

> keep My covenant, then you shall be My own possession from among all peoples; for all the earth is Mine; and you shall be to Me a kingdom of priests, and a holy nation.' These are the words which you shall speak to the sons of Israel." (Exo 19:3-6)

The elders heard the whole Covenant and then agreed. After that YHWH declared the Covenant to the whole assembly as above, complete with His signature of *thunders and lightnings...and the sound of an exceedingly loud shofar* and they also agreed. This is how the 12 Tribes of Israel entered into Covenant with YHWH at Sinai. Blessed be He forever and ever! Amen!

WHY THE WORLD HATES ISRAEL

Though there are exceptions, in the main, the world has never liked the fact that YHWH covenanted with Israel as one nation out of all nations to be His *own special possession from among all peoples* and to be *a kingdom of priests, and a holy nation*. This has always been perceived by the other nations of the world as favoritism, partiality and they resent it and refuse to accept it. In fact, the nations have persecuted Israel and are even now on a collision course with YHWH over precisely this issue.

WHY THE WORLD IS IN THE WRONG

While their rhetoric and actions target Israel their real dispute is with YHWH who chose Israel, to be *special*–not better, but *special*. The nations of the world are in the wrong in their wicked assessment of YHWH. As He said: *all the earth is Mine*. Since *all the earth* and everything in it is His then He is fully justified to do with it according to His own good pleasure with no need to answer to anyone. In choosing one nation out of all nations to have a unique status, He has acted within His rights as Creator of all. It is for the creature to conform to the will of the Creator, not for the Creator to adjust Himself to modern notions of the equality of nations. Indeed, He laughs at the nations in their ridiculous arrogance. Regardless of their schemes and political maneuverings, the Mosaic Covenant of Sinai eternally declares that all nations ARE NOT equal before Him, since His Covenant is with Israel <u>only</u>! (Exo 19:5)

When talk of the Covenant of Sinai arises the nations like to chide Israel for not obeying the Covenant. In their minds, Israel's failures negate the special status that the Covenant imparts to Israel.

Undoubtedly, the majority of Israel has not obeyed and all Israel has paid a heavy price because of it. Nevertheless, YHWH has made provision for Israel to yet honor the Covenant and to receive all its blessings as He intended from the start. He will not be thwarted in His original plan for the Covenant of Sinai by the sin of Israel any more than He will be thwarted from that original plan by the sin of the world. The sin of Israel is not at issue in Revelation 4:5 as YHWH repeats His Covenantal Signature of *lightnings and thunders and sounds.* Rather, the whole point of displaying that Signature before the High Court of Israel in Heaven is to declare that He is about to fulfill His obligations to faithful Israel according to that Holy Covenant. Though the words and actions of men and nations may fail, the Word and steadfastness of the Holy One of Israel cannot fail. Faithful Israelites, be of good cheer, for the day of Israel's Glory, that generations of our fathers have longed for, is now dawning!

BEFORE HIS THRONE

> 5b. There were seven lamps of fire burning **before his Throne**, which are the seven Spirits of God. 6. **Before the Throne** was something like a sea of glass, similar to crystal. (Rev 4:5b-6)

Chapter and verse numbering was not part of the original Scriptures, but was added later in translation. Sometimes the numbering is a convenience, but other times it actually obscures the correct flow of the text. This passage is a good example. *There were seven lamps of fire burning before his Throne, which are the seven Spirits of God* is included as an afterthought in verse 5. Actually, it is the start of an entirely new thought, after the segment introducing the 24 Elders, which segment should conclude with the Covenant Signature of verse 5a. Verse 5b and 6 should more correctly be translated as a new paragraph together under the same verse numbering. Why? Because they are both describing what Yochanan saw ***before the Throne*** after he viewed the 24 Elders.

WHY SIMPLE TRANSLATION ERRORS OCCUR

Why do translators make simple mistakes like this? The short answer is, even though they know Greek, they sometimes lack sufficient understanding of the message itself to translate the flow of the message exactly right. To illustrate; you are able to read English. Suppose you try to read something in English that expresses concepts or uses jargon you don't fully understand, say, a medical report, a legal paper, or a written description of an alien environment–such as heaven. Would you expect to pass on full comprehension of that material to a third party to whom you attempt to explain it? You might get it generally right, but not perfectly right. Why? More is required for full comprehension than just knowing the language a given concept is written in. Thus, we have this little foible in the numbering of Revelation 4:5b-6.

IN THE GAZE OF THE THRONE

Yochanan starts his description with the Throne. From there he mentions the next feature in his field of view, namely, the 24 Elder's throne-circle which stretches out on both sides of and forward of the Throne. Next, he describes those features beyond the 24 Elder's throne-circle, farthest from the Throne. Now we are talking about the area generally designated in the passage as ***before the Throne.***

Some might object, thinking *before the Throne* means directly in front of and next to the Throne. In other words, because the word *before* is used they would place this designated area even closer to the Throne than the 24 Elders. They are misled by the word *before. Before* has a greater sense of immediacy in English than the Greek word (G1799 *enopion*) it is used to translate. This Greek word literally means *before the face of* in the sense of being *in the sight of.* It has more to do with being the object of one's gaze than it has to do with proximity. *Before the Throne* more correctly means *in the gaze of the Throne.* In other words, *before the Throne* is the area of the Heavenly Court that the Throne's attention is focused upon. Of course, if the *One on the Throne* is focused upon something, so is everyone else who is present.

SEVEN LAMPS OF FIRE

Adding to this emphasis of focus, we have the *Seven Spirits of God* functioning as *seven lamps of fire* precisely in this area *before the Throne.* These are literally seven torches, not seven menorahs. Torches have a large flame to produce an abundance of light. This is purposeful. Why do you place the lamps as you do in any room of your house? Is it not so that you will have light to illuminate those things that command your attention in the room? That is exactly why the *seven lamps of fire* are placed as they are in the Heavenly Court.

SEVEN SPIRITS OF GOD IN ZECHARIAH

In Revelation 1:4 we were introduced to these *Seven Spirits of God*, but they do not originate there. This prophetic idea of the Spirit of God in seven manifestations originates in the prophetic Book of Zechariah. *These seven* are shown there in reference to the building of the Temple. There, instead of *seven lamps of fire* they are manifested as *seven eyes.* In Zechariah the *seven eyes* are said to be *the eyes of YHWH, which run back and forth through the whole earth.* Elsewhere we are told *YHWH's eyes are everywhere, keeping watch on the evil and the good.* Indeed, while YHWH is seated upon the Throne the *eyes of YHWH*, that is, His Holy Spirit, is spoken of as being in seven places at once. The Spirit is seeing everything *everywhere* at all times. (Zec 3:9, 4:10, Pro 15:3)

SEVEN EYES OR SEVEN LAMPS?

So why is the Spirit called *seven eyes* in Zechariah while being expressed as *seven lamps* in Revelation? As Messiah informs us: *The lamp of the body is the eye.* When YHWH Himself is seeing, as in Zechariah, His Spirit serves as *His eyes* by which He sees all. When He gives His Spirit that others may see what He is seeing, the Spirit illuminates the sight of the onlooker as does the light of a lamp. Seven lamps give total illumination in the Spirit. The seven lamps in the Heavenly Court are there for the 24 Elders and others in the Heavenly Court to see and understand what YHWH already sees and knows within the area of observation. What are the seven lamps illuminating in that area? (Mat 6:22, Psa 36:9)

Before the throne was something like a sea of glass, similar to crystal. This *sea* relates to the *molten sea* which was an immense and elaborately formed bronze basin placed between the sacrificial altar and the sanctuary, for the priests to wash in before officiating. Many of the elements of the Heavenly Court are found incorporated into the *molten sea,* though getting into that minutia here would be counter-productive to the bigger picture we are striving to present. Here is one brief account of the *molten sea*: "The molten sea was an immense semicircular vase, measuring seventeen and a half feet in diameter, and being eight and three-fourths feet in depth. This, at three and a half inches in thickness, could not weigh less than from twenty-five to thirty tons in one solid casting—and held from sixteen thousand to twenty thousand gallons of water. The brim was all carved with lily work or flowers; and oxen were carved or cut on the outside all round, to the number of three hundred; and it stood on a [bronze] pedestal of twelve oxen...when the vessel was filled with water, the whole weight would be about one hundred tons." (*Jamieson, Faussett and Brown Commentary, 1 Ki* 7:23-26, see also Exo 30:18, 1Ki 7:23-39, 2Ch 4:6)

This immense bronze wash basin was called a *sea* for its incredible size, being unmatched in the ancient world. The *sea* of the Heavenly Court is correspondingly much larger still. As the *molten sea* was placed beyond the altar but outside the sanctuary; so too with the *sea* of the Heavenly Court. In fact, the location of the *sea* confirms that these proceedings are not convened inside the Heavenly Sanctuary, but are convened in an intermediate position on the heaven-side of the altar of sacrifice, outside but leading into the sanctuary. The purpose of the *sea* is that the *Kingdom of Priests* may be fully cleansed and prepared before taking those last steps into the sanctuary at the appointed time, to officiate therein. (Rev 1:6, 5:10, 20:6)

STANDING ON THE SEA OF GLASS

The *sea* of the Heavenly Court is not specifically mentioned again in Revelation until Chapter 15. This is not the time to consider that in depth, except as it relates to our understanding of the *sea* in the Heavenly Court. Here is an excerpt:

> I saw something like a sea of glass mixed with fire, and those who overcame ... standing on the sea of glass, having harps of God. They sang the song of Moses, the servant of God, and the song of the Lamb. (Rev 15:2-3a)

This *sea* exists in heaven and on earth at the same time and is manifested somewhat differently in each place. On earth it is seen as *something like a sea of glass mixed with fire. Something like* means a prophetic apocalyptic symbol is being employed. The overcomers are seen standing on it, singing the *song of Moses* and *the song of the Lamb.* These overcomers, like Yochanan, are Israelites who keep the Covenant of Moses while also following the Lamb, the Messiah of Israel. They overcome in the midst of fiery trials in the earth, by which they are cleansed and refined. This prepares them for the Kingdom Priesthood that awaits them on the other side of the *sea of glass.* Notice that they stand <u>on</u> the *sea* not in the *sea.* As Messiah stood and walked on water so they are seen *standing on the sea of glass.* They do not sink nor are they consumed by the flames. Empowered by the Lamb's Blood, they actually walk out the Covenant of Moses, in Israel's name, making the way for YHWH to complete His side of that Covenant as well. They are the overcomers. Their walk through the *sea of glass mixed with fire* is so significant to the Heavenly Court that all eyes are focused on them. Indeed the entire Court is placed and arranged as it is to observe and facilitate these *overcomers* in their *sea* walk!

SIMILAR TO CRYSTAL

Before the Throne was something like a sea of glass, similar to crystal. There are no fiery trials on the heaven-side of the *sea,* though they can be observed through it. The word *crystal* (G2930 *krustallos*) actually means *a stone that looks like ice.* This is a large, clear, flat, hard, smooth surface–very much like your TV screen–and it is clear like *glass* for a very similar purpose. Truly, there is nothing new under the sun. Nineteen hundred years ago Yochanan used the language of his day to describe *something like* the ultimate big screen TV in heaven! Its purpose, as we have seen, is to view the walk of the overcomers *before the Throne,* even while they are in the earth.

THE BIG PICTURE

Consider this: the Heavenly Court is arranged a lot like your living room might be set up to watch the big game. You've got your big flat-screen TV centered against one wall of your living room–that's *something like a sea of glass, similar to crystal.* As host, you've got your big stuffed chair arranged directly across the room from the TV, that's *the Throne.* On either side of your chair around the room you have other seating for your friends to come over and watch the game on TV with you, that's the *24 Elder's thrones.* You have lamps placed strategically in the room to provide light for your friends, that's the *seven lamps.* At the appointed time your invited guests take their seats in your living room and all eyes are soon fixed on the TV screen to watch events in real time that are happening hundreds of miles away, that's the appointed time for the appointed events of the Judgment Meeting to begin on planet earth! Finally, there is the "big game" they are all focused on—more about that parallel contest as we proceed.

Now you know the layout of what Yochanan saw in the Heavenly Court. Countless thousands of Bible scholars have spent countless hours dissecting these verses, yet have never been able to put this little picture together. It wasn't time yet. Pretty simple, once you see it, isn't it?

JUDGMENT DAY

Court is Now in Session!

In the midst of the Throne and around the Throne were four live things full of eyes in front and behind.

The first live thing was like a lion,

and the second live thing like a young bull,

and the third live thing had the appearance like a man,

and the fourth live thing was like a flying eagle.

The four live things, each one of them having six wings, are full of eyes around and within.

They have no rest day and night, saying, “Holy, holy, holy is the Lord God, the Almighty, Who was and Who is and Who is to be!”

When the live things gave glory, honor, and thanks to Him who sat on the Throne, to Him who lives forever and ever, the twenty-four elders fell down before Him who sat on the Throne, and worshiped Him who lives forever and ever, and threw their crowns before the Throne, saying,

“Worthy are You, our Lord and God, the Holy One, to receive the glory, the honor, and the power, for You created all things, and because of Your will they existed, and were created!”

I saw, in the right hand of Him who sat on the Throne, a scroll written inside and outside, sealed shut with seven seals. (Rev 4:1-6b, 5:1)

So far, in our visit to the Heavenly Court, we have seen Israel very much at the center of the heavenly scene. Now, we draw back somewhat, to view a bigger picture originating from a much earlier time.

Yochanan directs our attention back to the Throne area once again. There we see *four live things full of eyes in front and behind.* Now, there's something you don't see everyday! Before we learn more about the *four live things* we observe their location. We are told that they are *in the midst of the Throne, and around the Throne.* How can they be in the midst of the Throne and around the Throne at the same time?

This would make no sense if we didn't already know about the platform the Throne was placed upon, as explained in Chapter four. *In the midst of the Throne* means the *four live things* are stationed in the midst of that Throne platform. Here the entire Throne area, including the Throne platform, is called *the Throne. Around the Throne* means they are also located around the Throne itself, around the seat where YHWH is seated. Being located directly next to the Throne, they are in the closest and most trusted position of all heavenly creatures. They are in the place reserved for the personal attendants of YHWH Himself! Who are these *live things* who enjoy this privileged position?

FOUR LIVE THINGS

Their name is translated from a Greek word (G2226 *zoon*) that literally means *live thing*. The KJV translates this as *beast.* This is an unfortunate translation since that term is easily confused by *the Beast* of Revelation 13, which is translated as such from another Greek word (G2342 *therion*) altogether. Other Bibles translate *zoon* as *living creature.* That's a lot better, but still not quite good enough. *Living creature* tends to put the emphasis on some sort of creature, which still directs us away from the crux of the meaning of the Greek word. Since both of the common translations here don't work, I have restored the literal meaning of *live thing* in my refinement of the translation. Since *thing* is ambiguous, this term leaves the emphasis on *live.* That's where the focus should be. The actual Greek word (G2226 *zoon*) is drawn from another Greek word (G2198 *zao*) that simply means *to live.* The emphasis of this term is on life itself in the act of living.

LIVE THINGS IN EZEKIEL

This term can be traced back to the Book of Ezekiel where the *four live things* are introduced in Scripture. In the Ezekiel vision we actually have the Throne of YHWH in motion, mounted upon the great chariot of YHWH. Stationed at the four wheels of Yah's great chariot are the *four live things.* A comparison of the Ezekiel vision with Revelation reveals some common elements and some differences. Differences include the different locations of the Throne in each respective apocalypse, as well as the differing circumstances of each respective Divine appearance. An element that does not significantly change is the name these four beings are called. The Hebrew root (H2416 *chay*) literally means *living, alive.* Once again the emphasis in the title of these four beings is on being *alive.*

WHY THESE FOUR ARE CALLED: *ALIVE!*

Consider the implications of this title. The title of *alive* came to these *four live things* because they were already *alive* when all the rest of the heavenly creatures were created. Therefore, they were called *alive* by all of the heavenly beings created after them. They are thus demonstrated to be the very first beings that YHWH ever created. Not being Divine, these *live things* are not eternally existent as YHWH is, but they are really old, older than everything and everyone else ever created in the universe! No wonder they are privileged to dwell i*n the midst of the Throne, and around the Throne* next to YHWH Himself. That's where they started out, and that's where YHWH has willed for them to dwell ever since.

FULL OF EYES

The *live things* are *full of eyes in front and behind.* In other words, they've seen it all. They have been *alive* from the beginning of the creation and they have seen all that has happened around the Throne through all of that time. They are the best witnesses creation can produce of events from the start of creation forward. Their worthiness as witnesses of universal issues being brought before the High Court is thus highlighted. Here, issues that pre-date Israel are being brought into view.

FOUR ANGELS OF THE PRESENCE

In Jewish apocalyptic literature, most notably in Enoch, these *four live things* are *Angels of the Presence,* because they stand directly in the presence of YHWH. In rank, they are Archangels. In other words, they are commanders over divisions of the heavenly hosts, not only to lead them in battle and function, but more especially to lead them in praise. They have names. Their names are *Michael, Gabriel, Uriel,* and *Raphael.* While these four are well established in Jewish literature, Christian interpreters largely ignore this information. I found a Christian interpreter who was an exception to that in my research, from the 1800s, who had some grasp of these facts. He states: "Four troops of ministering angels [are led in praise of] the holy blessed God: [The first leader] is Michael...the next is Gabriel... the third is Uriel...and the fourth is Raphael...the shechinah of the holy, blessed God is in the midst, and He Himself sits upon a throne high and elevated." (*Horae Hebraicae,* Christian Schoettgen)

While all of these four Angels of the Presence are named in Jewish apocalyptic books, only Michael and Gabriel are named in Scripture. Michael the Archangel is clearly the highest ranking of all the angels, being the leader of all the Heavenly Host. Then, of course, we have Gabriel, who was favored by YHWH to actually announce the coming of Messiah into the world. Honors this great are not bestowed upon lesser angels, as mighty and wonderful as all of them truly are. Such honors are reserved for those who dwell closest to the Throne. (Dan 8:16, 9:21, 10:13, 21, 12:1, Luk 1:19, 26, Jud 1:9, Rev 12:7)

A LION, A YOUNG BULL, A MAN, AND A FLYING EAGLE?

The four *live things* are represented with an appearance like a lion, like a young bull, like a man, and like an eagle, respectively. Rabbi Abin explains: "There are four which have principality in this world: among intellectual creatures, Man; among birds, the Eagle; among cattle, the Ox; and among wild beasts, the Lion: each of these has a kingdom and a certain magnificence, and they are placed under the throne of glory, Eze_1:10, to show that no creature is to exalt itself in this world, and that the kingdom of God is over all." (*Shemoth Rabba*, sec. 23, fol. 122, 4)

Rabbi Abin's explanation may seem to work in Ezekiel but it does not work in Revelation, since in Revelation these *live things* are not under, but are next to, the Throne. Actually, each of these four appearances is representative of four prime aspects that are characteristic of YHWH, upholding His Throne. These four prime aspects are also expressed in His creation. Together these four prime aspects provide a perfect balance of the Divine qualities. We see these four prime aspects in the *four live things*. Michael has an appearance like a lion, emphasizing the royal characteristics of justice, majesty, and authority. Gabriel is like a young bull. Bulls, of course, are noted for their tremendous power and vital energy. Uriel is like a man, emphasizing love, compassion, and intelligence. Raphael is like the flying eagle, representing swiftness, far-sightedness, and wisdom. These four *live things*, together, provide a perfect balance of Divine characteristics. This makes it possible for YHWH to always have one of them to turn to for most any assignment, depending upon the demands of that particular job. (Job 9:26, Due 32:4, Pro 14:4, 19:12, 20:2, Jer 49:42, Hab 1:8, Hos 11:4, Mic 6:8, Mat 5:48, Joh 15:13)

SIX WINGS

They each have six wings. The functionality of six wings is explained by the prophet Isaiah like this:

> With two he covered his face. With two he covered his feet. With two he flew. (Isa 6:2)

Though these beings are undoubtedly the most powerful created beings in the universe, in the presence of YHWH they cover their faces. Such is their great reverence before God. They cover their feet. They don't want any attention directed toward them in their service of YHWH, so they "cover their tracks," as the saying goes. They don't want us watching them. They don't want us seeing what they do. They want us to experience everything that comes forth from the Throne as coming from YHWH, not from them. Truly, their humility goes far beyond exemplary. (Jam 1:17, Rev 19:10, 22:8-9)

All of the interest and concern of the *four live things* is, and always has been, focused on the One on the Throne. As Yochanan says, *they have no rest day and night saying, "Holy, holy, holy, Lord God, the Almighty,*

Who was and is and Who is to be." He is the central focus of their entire existence and they are fully and completely in love with Him. They live to praise Him and to do His bidding and His trust in them is complete.

FULL OF EYES–AGAIN

The four live things, each one of them having six wings, are full of eyes around and within. A second time we are told about the eyes. Earlier we were told the *live things* are *full of eyes in front* (G1715 *emprosthen*) *and behind* (G3693 *opisthen*), literally meaning in front and in back. Now, the eyes are being described in relationship to the wings. The eyes are *around* (G2943 *kuklothen*) the wings and are also *within* (G2081 *esothen*), meaning inside the wings. Yochanan is going to the extreme to tell us the eyes cover every surface of these *live things*. Surely, you couldn't have better *eye*-witnesses than these.

All of this emphasis on these four being *full of eyes* is meant to be a big pointer toward what these four have seen. Yochanan knew exactly where that story is found, as would any Jew of his day. This is a reference to the Book of Enoch in which these four are named among *those who watch. Watch—full of eyes,* get it? (1 Enoch 20:1-8)

ABOUT THE BOOK OF ENOCH

Let's take a closer look at Enoch. Enoch is an apocalyptic book well known to all Jews of the 1st Century. Enoch was lost for centuries, until a copy translated from Greek was finally rediscovered in the 18th Century in Ethiopia. That Ethiopian copy, today called 1 Enoch, contains multiple words, phrases, passages and concepts found in the NT. As one scholar noted; "there are over one hundred comments in the New Testament which find precedence in the Book of Enoch." Rather than accept that Enoch could have been influential to the NT, scholars assumed that the Ethiopian Enoch had been fabricated using the many NT references.

That assumption has now been disproved. No less than ten Enoch scrolls have been found among the Dead Sea Scrolls (so-called because they were discovered near the shore of the Dead Sea in Israel). These scrolls are dated from two centuries before Christ, and nobody knows the antiquity of the source manuscripts before that. The Dead Sea Scroll fragments confirm that 1 Enoch is not a fabrication. The multiple words, phrases, passages and concepts found in the NT which are also in the book of 1 Enoch were original to Enoch–not the other way around! The same scholar quoted above explained: "It is hard to avoid the evidence that Jesus not only studied the book, but also respected it highly enough to allude to its doctrine and content." He also states; "The first Christians accepted the Book of Enoch as inspired, if not authentic." In Jude 1:14-15 Jude cites exact verses from Enoch, reproduced below, as authoritative. Given all of this evidence it is clear that Enoch was indeed revered as Scripture by early believers. Now that we understand that, let's focus on what Enoch actually wrote about. (Be aware that there is also a book called 2 Enoch which is of inferior quality and has not been authenticated. For that reason I have used 1 Enoch, but not 2 Enoch, as source material for this book. Quotes above are from *The Lost Book of Enoch*, Joseph B. Lumpkin, Blountsville: Fifth Estate Publishers, page viii.)

ENOCH SAW IT FIRST

Here are some excerpts from Enoch that indicate who Enoch was written for and what it is about:

> The words of the blessing of Enoch, wherewith he blessed the elect and righteous, who will be living in the day of tribulation, when all the wicked and godless are to be removed. And he took up his parable and said—Enoch a righteous man, whose eyes were opened by God, saw the vision of the Holy One in the heavens, which the angels showed me, and from them I heard everything, and from them I understood as I saw, but not for this generation, but for a remote one which is for to come. Concerning the elect I said, and took up my parable concerning them: The Holy Great One will come forth from His dwelling, And the eternal God will tread upon the earth, (even) on Mount Sinai, [And appear from

His camp] And appear in the strength of His might from the heaven of heavens.

... And behold! He cometh with ten thousands of His holy ones

To execute judgment upon all,

And to destroy all the ungodly:

And to convict all flesh

Of all the works of their ungodliness which they have ungodly committed,

And of all the hard things which ungodly sinners have spoken against Him. (Enoch 1:1-4, 9)

FOR THE ELECT...IN THE DAY OF TRIBULATION

Enoch states that he was not writing for his own generation, but was writing for *the elect and righteous,* which will be *living in* ***the day of tribulation, when all the wicked and godless are to be removed***. How relevant is that to what Yochanan is writing about in the Revelation?

We also note that Enoch was favored with a ***vision of the Holy One in the heavens.*** Is not Revelation chapter four, which we are now studying, a description of a very similar experience had by Yochanan? Do you think Yochanan would have been struck by the similarity between Enoch's experience and his own?

Finally, note that Enoch writes about the time when YHWH comes to ***execute judgment upon all*** and to ***convict all flesh of all the works of their ungodliness*** and ***of all the hard things which ungodly sinners have spoken against Him***. Indeed, *judgment* and *convicting the ungodly* is what the Judgment Court in Heaven is convened to accomplish!

ENOCH'S OLD, SAD STORY OF REBELLION

Now let's consider how the four Angels of the Presence figure into this. In the Book of Enoch, we are given a window into the era before the Great Flood of Noah. There we find that mankind once had much more contact with angelic beings than they do now. That contact has been greatly reduced since the Flood for a very good reason. Back then there was a rebellion in which many angels sinned through illicit contact with mankind. Many actually abandoned their place and duty in heaven to cohabit with women on earth. They produced hybrid offspring called *nephilim* who never should have been born. This created a genetic crisis in the earth. The fallen ones also brought technology into the earth that man was not ready to handle. All of this accelerated violence and all manner of evil in the world. This is confirmed in Genesis. However, Enoch gives a lot more detail. (Gen 6, see also my book, *Holy Order Restored*)

MEN IMPLORE THE FOUR TO MAKE THEIR SUIT

Enoch writes:

> And then Michael, Uriel, Raphael, and Gabriel looked down from heaven and saw much blood being shed upon the earth, and all lawlessness being wrought upon the earth. And they said one to another: 'The earth made without inhabitant cries the voice of their cryingst up to the gates of heaven.
>
> And now to you, the holy ones of heaven, the souls of men make their suit, saying, "Bring our cause before the Most High."'
>
> And they said to the Lord of the ages: 'Lord of lords, God of gods, King of kings, and God of the ages, the throne of Thy glory (standeth) unto all the generations of the ages, and Thy name holy and glorious and blessed unto all the ages! Thou hast made all things, and power over all things hast Thou: and all things are naked and open in Thy sight, and Thou seest all things, and nothing can hide itself from Thee. (Enoch 9: 1-5)

We see here that as this crisis developed *Michael, Uriel, Raphael, and Gabriel* looked on. These four are mentioned together often in Enoch. Michael is listed first while the order in which the others are listed varies. Always, however, these are the highest ranking angels who are closest to YHWH. They saw the whole rebellion unfold, in fact, from Eden forward, so that the inhabitants of the earth bring their *suit* to them imploring them, in turn, to bring the case before YHWH.

TEMPORARY MEASURES–THEN DOCKETED FOR JUDGMENT DAY

In due course the rebellion was temporarily set back by means of the Great Flood. In those days the Four were sent to restrict the fallen angels and their offspring until a future Day of Judgment at the end of the age, in which all of these issues would be finally resolved. Enoch points forward to that *Day of Judgment* numerous times, as in this passage:

> The Most High will arise on that Day of Judgment to execute great judgment amongst sinners. (Enoch 100:4, Compare 2Pe 2:4, 9)

The judgment of the rebellion has been pending all this time, waiting for the end of the age to arrive, just as Enoch prophesied that it would. Since the Flood the rebellion has been ripening, developing to its fullness, in both heaven and earth. Through all of this the *four live things* have been watching. (2Pe 3:7-9)

From a Hebraic perspective, Yochanan's emphasis on the *four live things full of eyes* is suggestive of this entire drama from Enoch. The case of the rebellion, placed into the hands of the four Angels of the Presence by *suit* of men, is now brought, in Revelation, before the Judgment Court for a final resolution, since the end of the age has arrived. All the issues raised by the rebellion in heaven and on earth, from the very beginning right down to the present day, are up for judgment in the Judgment Court. The Heavenly Judgment Court, convened, indicates the *Day of Judgment* has arrived. *Day of Judgment* and *Judgment Day* are equivalent, interchangeable terms.

THE DECLARATION

Now, let's take a closer look at the words of the *live things* and how the 24 *Elders* also play into this.

> They have no rest day and night, saying, "Holy, holy, holy is the Lord God, the Almighty, Who was and Who is and Who is to be!"
>
> When the live things gave glory, honor, and thanks to Him who sat on the Throne, to Him who lives forever and ever, the twenty-four elders fell down before Him who sat on the Throne, and worshiped Him who lives forever and ever, and threw their crowns before the Throne, saying,
>
> "Worthy are You, our Lord and God, the Holy One, to receive the glory, the honor, and the power, for You created all things, and because of Your will they existed, and were created!" (Rev 4:8b-11)

Did you notice how similar these words are to the words of the Angels of the Presence, as quoted from Enoch above? There are some differences, too. Enoch does not include the 24 Elders. That makes sense, because the 24 Elders had not yet come into being before the Flood, the time period in which the Enoch events took place. In Revelation, the 24 Elders take up the cry of the *live things,* repeating the affirmation of YHWH as being Creator, declaring His holiness, glory, and power over all His creation. The 24 *Elders* are actually said to be joining in with the *live things* in these declarations.

PERSPECTIVE ON THE DECLARATION OF THE FOUR LIVE THINGS

As we consider these declarations as they originate in Enoch, we get some perspective on them. In Enoch, those worshipful words, that people today see only as simple praises of YHWH, are actually much more than that.

They are spoken as a response to what the Four were seeing, *all lawlessness being wrought upon the earth.* This, along with the cries bringing *suit* against the rebellion, prompts the affirmations of YHWH by the four Angels of the Presence. These praises are meant as an indictment against the ungodly, declaring YHWH to be in the right!

AN OPEN AND SHUT CASE

O Lord, You are worthy to receive glory and honor and power, because You created all things, and for Your will they are and were created is thus more than simple worship. It is also a legal argument being brought before the Judgment Court. It is a statement of principle demonstrating why the rebels are in the wrong. YHWH is the Creator and the rebels, like all creation, were created for His purposes, not their own. Yet, they have abandoned His will and have denied Him *the glory and honor and power* in their lives of which *He is worthy.* This is a classic example of what any court of law today considers a *prima facie* case. This is a case that "at first sight" is obvious. *Res ipsa loquitur* is also a legal term that applies well to this declaration. *Res ipsa loquitur* essentially means "the thing speaks for itself." It signifies that further details are unnecessary; the proof of the case is self-evident. (http://www.answers.com/Res ipsa loquitur)

THE INDICTMENT OF THE REBELS ESTABLISHED

The indictment against the rebels is thus established before the Heavenly Court as self-evident, with no need for further proof or discussion. Besides, from the point of view of the 1st Century Messianic reader of Revelation, this evidence has already been adequately supplied by Enoch and elsewhere and therefore does not require repetition here. That is not necessarily so for modern readers. This is one of the many places in Revelation where we must fill in the blanks left by Yochanan, which he assumed his readers could readily fill in from common knowledge of other Hebrew apocalyptic sources. What was common knowledge then has long since passed out of the collective consciousness of the believing community.

A DAMNABLE CRIME

Let's take a closer look at the key statement here.

> Worthy are You, our Lord and God, the Holy One, to receive the glory, the honor, and the power, for You created all things, and because of Your will they existed, and were created! (Rev 4:11)

That YHWH is *worthy to receive glory, honor, and power* from all His creatures is established by the fact that He created them. That means all creatures belong to Him and are morally bound to fulfill the purpose for which He made them. This is the prime fact of Scripture and the fundamental reason why it is evil to choose not to serve and obey God. To choose to rebel is to deny YHWH what is rightfully His. This theme of perfect obedience to God as Creator is consistent throughout Scripture as the fundamental issue of the universe. This is the watershed issue that separates the righteous from the wicked. Notice here that the primary issue is not about us–it is about Him. He is worthy of perfect service and obedience from all of His creatures and He is not getting it. That is a gross sin and a damnable crime that must be set right. It is for our sakes that He has patiently endured the outrage of rebellion until now, that some of us might take the opportunity to repent. (Gen 17:1, Due 18:13, Exo 19:5, Psa 7:9, 11, 37:17, Pro 11:8, 12:5, 15:29, 21:18, 29:16, 3:17, Mal 3:18, Col 1:10, 1Th 2:12)

IS THIS YOU?

What are the implications of this for your life? Many of us think it is fine for us to put our own interests first in our lives so long as we offer token works of worship to God. The hour in church, the contribution to our favorite cause, the incidental good works we do, are sometimes regarded as little favors we do for God that keep things smoothed over with Him–as we mostly go on doing as we please. If this is you, stop kidding yourself. You can do no little favors for God because you already <u>owe</u> Him everything. That you throw a few tokens His way does not make up for the fact that you have reserved everything else for yourself. That is rebellion. To do right toward Him, you must put Him first in all things. (Pro 21:27, Mat 22:38, Luk 14:27, 33, Rev 3:15-16)

24 ELDERS CAST THEIR CROWNS

That is admittedly a struggle for fallen mankind. That is what is so encouraging about the 24 Elders casting their crowns before Him and acknowledging His claim to their lives by the very words we are here discussing. Their crowns were obtained because they had overcome the tendencies of this rebellious world. They completed their course as overcomers, serving YHWH with their whole being. By casting their crowns before Him they acknowledge, not only that He is worthy, but also that He has empowered them to overcome, so that ultimately even those crowns come from Him! We learn from the 24 Elders that He has made the impossible possible for us, if only we will surrender our will and put our full trust in Him. (1Co 9:25-27, Jam 1:12, 1Pe 5:4, 1Jo 4:4)

THE MORAL IMPERATIVE IN THE CRY OF THE RIGHTEOUS

The cry of the 24 Elders is the cry of all of the righteous. In worshipping Him and living for Him we declare in the midst of this wayward world that He is worthy! He is our Creator. He is deserving of our worship and our very lives. This constant cry of the righteous raises a question. It's not that we even intend to bring up the question. However, the cry of the righteous raises the question before Him nonetheless. That question is: What about all of the ones that do not give Him the worship and service He is worthy to receive? Since we have surrendered all to Him it follows that we look to Him for everything. Among those things are righteous judgments, because only He can bring such righteous judgments to pass. Only He can set things right. So, when the righteous say to Him, "You are worthy" He also hears: "What are you going to do about the ones that don't treat You as worthy?" (Psa 1:5-6, 35:24, Eze 7:27, Act 4:19-20, 1Co 11:32)

He is righteous. From His standpoint when He looks upon the righteous and He sees them honoring Him, He feels a moral imperative to meet their need. He feels the call to make a righteous judgment to set things right in the universe regarding those who are polluting the universe with rebellion.

That's the gut level interchange we're encountering in Revelation 4:11. This one statement is the overarching issue before the Divine Court. The moral imperative that naturally follows from this declaration is that rebellion must now be judged and eradicated. (Psa 11:6, 31:17, 34:15-22)

REBELS DENY YHWH HIS DUE

This brings us to satan, the fallen angels, and the world in rebellion. They do not acknowledge YHWH as worthy of the glory, honor, and power in their lives. They do not acknowledge His rights as Creator. They prefer to seek their own will instead, making each of them a god unto themselves. They express the attitude: "Who needs a Creator? I will take care of myself." They behave as if every resource they can get their hands on is theirs, not His. (Psa 9:17, 10:4, 13, 14:1, 96:1-13)

Here we see two opposing concepts in the universe, representing two possible choices, as regards the claims of YHWH as Creator. There are the righteous, which stand with YHWH in ascribing to Him His due. Then there are satan, the fallen angels, and the world in rebellion, who continue on in a state of rebellion against YHWH the Creator. These are the only possible sides to choose from. The time allowed to make a final choice is closing fast! (Psa 100:1-5)

Realize, this is more than just an intellectual difference. The Rebellion, besides being an offense against God, has also disturbed the harmony of the universe for a very long time. It is, in fact, the source of numerous crimes against all the righteous in heaven and on earth and even crimes against the creation itself. The rebels have muddied the stream for everyone, not just themselves. (Job 24:13-17, Rom 8:22, Rev 11:18)

THE WALK OF THE RIGHTEOUS CONVICTS THE WICKED

The only defense the rebels have is to say that they are no different than anyone else. Thus satan and the wicked accuse the righteous of serving YHWH because of the blessings they receive from Him, rather than out of true love for Him and for what is right. If the righteous are only acting out of self-interest then, in the final analysis, there is no difference between the righteous and the wicked–since both are putting themselves first. This was the great charge of the accuser before the Throne regarding Job. This charge is made against all of the righteous.

This explains the trials of the overcomers being viewed in the great *Crystal Sea*. The righteous have a role in this Judgment Court too. They are given an opportunity, in the face of the worst the rebels can do, to answer the accuser by their own faith and deeds, just as Job did, to prove their love for YHWH before all onlookers. Their righteous walk in the face of every trial convicts the ungodly of their wickedness. Never forget that your walk is being both observed and recorded in Heaven! (Job 1:7-11, 1Co 4:9, Heb 11:7, Rev 12:10-11)

Now, let's summarize the principle issues before the Court.

SUMMARY OF THE CASE NOW BEFORE THE JUDGMENT COURT

Fact #1. Revelation 4:11-YHWH is worthy to receive glory, honor, and power by virtue of being Creator.

> **Indictment #1.** satan, the fallen angels, and the world in rebellion, do not acknowledge YHWH as worthy of the glory, honor, and power in their lives. Instead, they behave as gods unto themselves.

Fact #2. Revelation 4:11-YHWH owns all creation: *You created all things, and because of Your will they existed, and were created!*

> **Indictment #2.** satan, the fallen angels, and the world in rebellion, claim effective ownership of the creation, for themselves, selfishly grabbing all they can.

CHARGES AGAINST THE REBELLION INCLUDE:

1. Sin against the Creator.
2. The righteous motives of YHWH have been impinged.
3. Introduction of sin, death, and suffering into the world.

4. Even the righteous are infected with sin and death by the Rebellion.
5. Destructive effect of sin on the created universe.
6. Hostility and persecution by the rebels against all the righteous, especially against Israel.
7. The obedience of the righteous out of love of YHWH has been impinged.
   (More information about these issues can be found in my book, *Holy Order Restored*, ISBN-13: 978-0-9679471-1-2.)

OTHER FACTS REQUIRING CLOSURE

Fact #3: YHWH has made covenant promises that must be fulfilled. All these covenants involve Israel. (This is the principle reason why the 24 Elders of Israel are present at the Judgment, to represent the interests of all Israel.)

Fact #4: It follows from the perfect and holy nature of YHWH that He must resolve all issues raised by the Rebellion and must set all matters right in His creation. (This will satisfy all issues raised in the sight of the *four live things* from the foundation of the world.)

RESPONSE OF THE KING

All of the facts, indictments, and bad results of the Rebellion have now been placed before YHWH as the King of the Universe and as the Creator. How will He resolve all of these issues, returning the universe to a perfect state? Revelation 5:1 reveals His astonishing response.

> "I saw, in the right hand of Him who sat on the Throne, a scroll written inside and outside, sealed shut with seven seals." (Rev 5:1)

As commonly translated, He has a "book" in His right hand. Rarely if ever do interpreters offer more than a guess explaining what the "book" actually is. Some assume it's the Book of Life. No, that comes later. Some say, "This is the title deed to the earth." Nonsense! As we've seen, the Creator needs no such deed to secure His Divine ownership of the Creation. Other's say,

"This is His last will and testament." That is also nonsense. The Creator lives forever. He will never have use of a last will and testament, as do dying mortals. Some get a little closer to the truth saying, "This is His Eternal Purpose." It's fair to say what He holds in His right hand is related to His Eternal Purpose, but that's not really what this book is either.

WE DON'T HAVE TO GUESS

With Yochanan's observation of the Heavenly Court that has now been shared with you there is no longer a need to guess what the "book" is. Let's review. We observed that the Throne is located in an area of Heaven dedicated to Judgment. That Judgment Court is, in many ways, similar to the Judgment Porch of the king of Israel. At the Judgment Porch, the king declared his judgments affecting the subjects of his kingdom. Very often those judgments were written down as law in the form of a royal decree. This scene in Revelation follows that same pattern. In Revelation, this is the King of the Universe sitting upon the Throne of Judgment and it is His duty to judge the case brought before the Court. The case has been brought before the Court by the *four live things* and by the 24 *Elders* on behalf of all the righteous of heaven and earth and especially on behalf of Israel.

HIS ROYAL DECREE

The "book" is the King's response–His righteous judgment, in the form of His Royal Decree.

Now let's consider what is different about the "book" compared to the typical decree of an ancient king. When a case involving the interests of the kingdom came before the king, he would deal with the problem by way of a royal decree. Usually the king would consult his advisors, and then he would deliberate on the matter himself. After all available information had been considered, he would formulate his judgment and would issue a royal decree. Normally, he would dictate the decree to his scribe, but he might write it out himself. His decree would be intended to embody a comprehensive plan to fully deal with all aspects of the case–his full solution to the problem, if you will. (2Ch 30, Ezr 5-7, Est 1:20, 3:15, 4:3,8, 9:13, Psa 2:7, 148:6)

The "book" in the right hand of YHWH is His Royal Decree containing His comprehensive judgment and solution to all aspects of the Rebellion! The astonishing thing is, He doesn't have to gather information from advisors or deliberate about the case. Neither does He need to call a scribe over to write out the decree. Why? Because He has had the decree already in completion before the Court was ever in session. In fact, ***the decree was completed and in His right hand before the Rebellion ever began!***

NOT A BOOK–A SCROLL

While the Greek word (G975 *biblion*) here is usually translated as "book" it actually means a roll, a scroll. We have restored that translation to our refinement of the text above. The Scroll is *in His right hand.* In the Greek that's literally *lying upon His right hand.* His hand is extended and opened and the Scroll is lying upon the palm of His hand. He's offering it as the solution to the case! In this action He is as much as saying, "This is my Royal Decree. Here is My Judgment that will solve all problems arising from the Rebellion."

WITHIN AND BEHIND

We notice that it is written *on the inside and the outside,* literally in the Greek that's *within and behind.* That terminology fits a scroll but not a book. The fact that the Scroll is written on the back is unusual. Normally scrolls were not written on both sides, they were only written on one side. Then, when the scroll was rolled up the writing was protected. Certainly, this scroll is not written on both sides because YHWH does not have enough writing material, being the Owner of the universe. It's this way to make a point. If you have one piece of paper and you write on the front, then you write on the back, nobody can add anything more to it, nor do they need to. Your document is complete. That's the idea with the Royal Decree. It is full and sufficient. It doesn't need anything added to it. Neither should anything be taken away from it. It's exactly complete and perfect to accomplish its purpose. (Eze 2:10)

A PERFECT SOLUTION IN HAND!

Consider the implications of that. He's got one decree that is full, complete and totally sufficient to straighten out this mess that we are all suffering from. Now, as one of His servants, I rejoice in that. Despite all of the problems that this world faces and that we face in this world, our Father has already designed a perfect solution that answers all of it. When we're focused on the issue of rebellion and that He is worthy, it doesn't matter what happens to us, because He's worthy and He's got the answer and He's going to set it right. He's not going to do that without taking us into consideration. We may have to suffer until the Judgment is concluded, but He suffered a much longer time than we have. Really, all of creation is suffering because of the Rebellion, so it is not strange that we suffer as well. However, the suffering of the righteous is not without hope of something better. The Royal Decree means there is hope of something better–and it is on its way!

SEALED WITH SEVEN SEALS

The Royal Decree is *sealed with seven seals*. In the ancient world, a king's decree was sealed with the king's seal. This required the use of the king's signet impressed in wax or clay, sealing the document.

The seal served three purposes.

1. The seal served as authentication of the document.
2. The seal closed the document, guaranteeing it to be complete.
3. The seal protected the document from tampering. No one would dare tamper with a document having the king's seal!

The seven seals on the Royal Decree of YHWH mean you can multiply the intensity of each of the three purposes of a king's seal by a factor of seven. This Royal Decree, while being both supremely authentic and supremely complete, is also supremely closed to ALL unauthorized persons. That means that no matter how hard you study, no matter how much you dig, you will not understand what is in that Royal Decree, unless that is specifically released to you from above. This scroll can never be opened by the mere intellectual ability of man. It is seven times sealed! (Psa 50:1-6, Isa 55:7-8, Rom 8:7, Jam 3:17)

NOT LIKE THE PICTURES

Perhaps you have seen illustrations of this Scroll with seven seals placed in a neat row along the leading edge of the page. That is not how the seals of the Royal Decree are configured. The seven seals are placed successively upon the volume as it is rolled up, so that each opening of the Scroll reveals the Scroll only so far as the next seal allows. To go further, the next seal must be opened, and so on, through each of the seven seals. The first seal not only closes the first segment of the Scroll, it also serves to close the entire volume. The opening of the first seal leads to all the others being progressively opened as well.

A PROGRESSIVE JUDGMENT ON AN APPOINTED SCHEDULE

The progressive nature of the seals on the Scroll relate to the Divine timing. There is a precise appointed time for each seal to be opened, releasing the judgment events of each respective seal. All of this is progressing according to His Divine order and CANNOT BE CHANGED. From down on the earth the unsealing of His judgments looks and will look chaotic, but from the standpoint of heaven everything is moving according to His judgments to eventuate in His perfect will. (Psa 75:2, Dan 8:19, 11:35, Mal 3:6)

Here is an awesome and reassuring fact about the Scroll: This complex document was all prepared ahead of time and sealed up with each segment to be released in its own pre-ordained way and time. Nobody saw that happen. The *live things* have witnessed everything from the start of creation forward. Yet, they first saw the Scroll as already completed and sealed. This can only mean that they weren't around when the Scroll was prepared, before the creation of the world. That is really quite staggering. Before the creation of the world, YHWH already had His Royal Decree containing His righteous judgments ready, in every detail, to set this whole mess right. You simply cannot surprise the One who knows the end from the beginning. Truly, He is worthy! (Act 15:13, Heb 4:3, 1Pe 1:18-21, Isa 46:10)

Most think of the Day of Judgment as the actual day on which the punishments will fall. The word *day* does not require a 24-hour period, since, in the Scriptures, a 'day' may simply mean a period of time. Also, we have learned that *judgment* means much more than only punishment. It is more correctly the progressive process in which hearts are tried and eventually brought to an appropriate outcome. The progressive nature of the Day of Judgment is well demonstrated by the progressive nature of the Scroll. The Day of Judgment is an appointed period of time in which the judgments prepared ahead of time by YHWH progressively unfold. Realize that the Day of Judgment started at the moment the Judgment Court sat to hear the case in Heaven. Now, all *must happen*. If we enter into His timing, His order, and His ways, the judgments released at the opening of each seal will not be the chaos for us that they will surely be for the rest of the world.

HURRY UP–AND WAIT

Well, great! The solutions are all there already, in the Scroll! YHWH is extending the Scroll on His right hand. Somebody grab that Scroll and let's get on with this!

Not so fast. There is a problem, a tragic problem. It's enough to make a grown man weep.

THE LION OF JUDAH STANDS UP

The Lamb's Day of Power

The Judgment Court of Heaven is now in session. Judgment Day has begun. Indictments against the Rebellion have been brought before the Court. King YHWH responds. He extends His right hand, offering a Scroll sealed with seven seals. This is His Royal Decree detailing out His righteous Judgment. It contains the complete solution to the Rebellion and all of its horrible effects.

A CALL GOES FORTH

Next, a call goes forth from Michael, Archangel and Chief Courtier to the Throne.

> Who is worthy to open the scroll, and to break its seals? (Rev 5:2)

This too follows the manner of ancient kings. From ancient times a royal decree is put into force by placing it in the hand of an agent of the throne who is worthy; able to fully execute all that is contained therein. The call here goes out from Heaven for such a worthy Person to step forward as the Agent of the Throne, to open the Royal Decree, to break its seals, including to fully implement all that is in it according to the Divine Plan. (Gen 41:33-44, Ezr 7:13-17)

Here we have a problem. This job requires extraordinary qualifications.

> No one in heaven above, or on the earth, or under the earth, was able to open the scroll, or to look in it. (Rev 5:3)

WEEPING IN HEAVEN

What a letdown! The solution to all the trouble in the Universe is offered—but there is nobody worthy and able to implement the solution. Yochanan's deep emotional response captures something of the tragedy of this drama.

> And I wept much, because no one was found worthy to open the scroll, or to look in it. (Rev 5:4)

Imagine that! Yochanan was weeping in Heaven. He immediately felt the deeply tragic truth: Apart from a worthy individual able to open and to implement that Scroll, the situation for all creation is absolutely hopeless.

OUR JEWISH CHAMPION IN HEAVEN

Just when all appeared to be lost Yochanan was encouraged to look upon the Champion of Israel.

> One of the elders said to me, "Don't weep. Behold, the Lion who is of the Tribe of Judah, the Root of David, has overcome; He who opens the scroll and its seven seals." (Rev 5:5)

This dramatic pronouncement illustrates the absolute necessity of Messiah. Without Him, there is no hope. Even though YHWH sits on the Throne, even though He offers a perfect judgment plan sufficient to restore the creation to perfection, ultimately Messiah is at the center of that plan and He is absolutely essential to it. He cannot be replaced by anyone else, because no one else is worthy and capable of mastering the task but Him.

Because He lives, we have hope. We don't have to be overcome by the futility of the world. There is One Who is worthy to open the Scroll and its seven seals. He's the Lion, the Lion of the Tribe of Judah. Don't miss this. There is a Jew in Heaven, and He alone is worthy to open the Scroll.

LION OF THE TRIBE OF JUDAH FORETOLD

This harkens back to the Book of Genesis where Jacob, renamed Israel, prophesied the future, speaking his patriarchal blessing to each of his 12 sons. He prophesied that a worthy "Lion" of the line of Judah would arise with the right to rule. This was a promise made to Judah, one of those 24 Elders found in Revelation, taking part in these judgment proceedings in Heaven. In fact, I would expect the Elder who announced the worthy *Lion Who is of the Tribe of Judah* to Yochanan was Judah himself!

Let's read the promise that Judah held dear unto its fulfillment.

> Judah, your brothers will praise you. Your hand will be on the necks of your enemies. Your father's sons will bow down before you. Judah is a lion's cub. From the prey, my son, you have gone up. He stooped down, he crouched as a lion, Who will rouse him up? The scepter will not depart from Judah, nor the ruler's staff from between his feet, until He comes to whom it belongs. To Him will the obedience of the peoples be. (Gen 49:8-10)

Not only would the staff of rulership remain in the lion-like Tribe of Judah, but, in time, One Jewish Lion would come to whom it (the rulership) belongs. That is, One would come Who is worthy to command the obedience of the peoples.

THE PUZZLE RAPIDLY FILLS IN

We should be seeing a pattern of fulfillment here by now. This Revelation Judgment Day is much like a puzzle board of prophetic Scripture. All prophecies of Scripture still remaining unfulfilled will be rapidly brought into place, quickly completing the puzzle of the ages. In Revelation, we see one after the other of such prophecies set in place in rapid succession. Many are alluded to which are not specifically cited. Take, for example, Genesis, chapter 49. Revelation is claiming a fulfillment of that prophecy in the last days regarding *the Lion of the Tribe of Judah.*

ELEVEN MORE LAST DAYS PROPHECIES

This begs the question: What about the prophecies uttered on the same day, at the same time, to the other eleven brothers? When we consider how all of these prophecies were introduced you will see that is a fair question.

> Jacob called to his sons, and said: "Gather yourselves together, that I may tell you that which will happen to you in the last days." (Gen 49:1 See KJV)

Jacob did not prophesy to only Judah that day, but to all twelve of *his sons*. The prophecy concerning Judah is but one-twelfth of the entire prophecy uttered on that occasion. Jacob told his sons, *I'll tell you what will befall you in the last days*. Since he speaks of *the last days*, he's not talking about what will befall them personally. He is speaking of the future of each of their twelve tribes.

THE DESTINY OF ISRAEL

The implications of this prophecy for the Twelve Tribes of Israel are profound. While Christians mostly ignore this, Jewish scholars understand that nothing short of the destiny of Israel is embodied in these verses. "Nachmanides says, according to the sense of all their writers, the last days here are the days of the Messiah; and in an ancient writing of the Jews it is said (x), that "Jacob called his sons, because he had a mind to reveal the end of the Messiah," i.e. the time of his coming; and Abraham Seba (y) observes, that this section is "the seal and key of the whole Torah" and "of all the prophets prophesied of, unto the days of the Messiah."" (*Gill's Exposition of the Entire Bible,* (x) Zohar in Gen. fol. 126. 1. (y) Tzeror Hammor, fol. 57. 4. & 58. 1.)

In the Jewish world, it has long been understood that *the last days* Jacob speaks of in Genesis 49 are the days at the end of the age that will usher in the coming of Messiah to take up His Kingdom in Jerusalem. As shown above, the Rabbis have recognized that both the Torah and the Prophets point forward to the fulfillment of the destiny of Israel in the *last days,* as uttered by Jacob to his twelve sons. That Yochanan makes reference to this prophecy of Genesis 49 in introducing the worthy Lion of Judah is profound. He is asserting in this scene that the *last days*, the days of Messiah, are now upon us. Further, in asserting that the prophecy made to Judah is here fulfilled, he is likewise asserting that the rest of the prophecy regarding all Twelve Tribes of Israel is about to be fulfilled as well, in these *last days*. The Twelve Tribes of Israel are about to fulfill their destiny! This certainly adds further meaning to the presence of the 24 Elders of Israel at these proceedings. This should also be another strong indication of just how pivotal we can expect Israel to be in the unfolding of Scroll events still ahead.

ROOT OF DAVID

The *Lion of the Tribe of Judah* is also *the Root of David*. This is a reference to the Davidic Covenant and Messiah's Davidic connection. This Davidic association is a deep subject requiring a book in this series of its own. We are merely pointing out at this time that a physical connection with Israel is once again brought into view. (Psa 118:19-23; 110:1, Isa 11, Mar 12:35-37, Rev 22:16)

The prophets foretold the Davidic Lion of Judah coming to set things right for Israel, and the world, in the *last days*. This Commanding Figure is the Messianic persona that Jews have traditionally acknowledged. Many of them have found it impossible, however, to reconcile that impressive picture of the magnificent Lion with what Yochanan saw next.

THE LION IS A LAMB

> I saw in the midst of the Throne and of the four live things, and in the midst of the elders, a Lamb standing, as though it had been slain. (Rev 5:6a)

Lions are powerful, dangerous, and majestic. Lambs are wooly, soft, gentle and apparently harmless. Here we are confronted with a paradox. Our mighty Lion is a...Lamb! How can this be?

This can be because lambs have one other important characteristic in Scripture. Lambs are used for sacrifice.

PASSOVER LAMB

That is the case here. This is a Lamb appearing *as though it had been slain.* The marks of its sacrifice are still to be seen. To Yochanan the Jew, this Lamb symbol relates to the Passover lamb. Remember the story of the deliverance of Israel from Egypt? The firstborn of man and beast throughout the land were all to be slain that night by the Angel of Death. However, deliverance was offered to Israel from this doom by way of the Passover lamb. In each home of the sons of Israel, blood of the Passover lamb was to be applied to the lintel and doorposts. The Angel of Death would see that blood, and "pass over" that house. Thus, the name of that memorial event: Passover.

Passover was instrumental in freeing Israel from bondage, to become a free nation. Israel was delivered out of Egypt that very night. Passover is to be kept as an everlasting memorial each year by Israel, that's how vital Passover is to the life of the nation. By contrast, most Christians have not kept Passover since the 4th Century. This reference to the Passover lamb is thus meaningful primarily to Israel. Messiah is the ultimate Passover Lamb of Israel. (1Co 5:7)

CUT OFF FOR THE DISOBEDIENCE OF MY PEOPLE, ISRAEL

In Isaiah 53, the Hebrew prophet Isaiah speaks of *our, we, everyone, us,* and finally, *my people.* To whom do these expressions correctly refer? Isaiah was clearly referring to his fellow Israelites by these expressions. Here is an excerpt from those verses:

> But He was pierced for our transgressions. He was crushed for our iniquities. The punishment that brought our peace was on Him; and by His wounds we are healed. All we like sheep have gone astray. Everyone has turned to his own way; and YHWH has laid on Him the iniquity of us all.

He was oppressed, yet when He was afflicted He didn't open His mouth. As a lamb that is led to the slaughter, and as a sheep that before its shearers is mute, so He didn't open his mouth.

He was taken away by oppression and judgment; and as for His generation, who considered that He was cut off out of the land of the living and stricken for the disobedience of My people? (Isa 53:5-18)

ONLY A LION COULD BE THIS LAMB

YHWH promised to send Israel *a lamb* to be *pierced for our transgressions. Our transgressions* means *Israel's transgressions* here. Who is that Lamb? Who could possibly have the incredible strength of character to allow Himself to be *a lamb that is led to the slaughter*, to be *stricken for the disobedience of* Israel, without so much as saying a word in protest? No man has such strength, except for One: the *Lion of the Tribe of Judah*—Israel's Messiah. This is none other than Y'shua Messiah, the Lamb of God, and the Savior of Israel. Because He has obeyed YHWH even to death, and has ransomed Israel (and all who are joined to Israel) with His own blood, He alone *is worthy to open the Scroll, and to break its seals.*

FOCUS ON ISRAEL

Notice when Messiah comes into view. In Revelation 5, the primary focus remains on Israel. The rest of the world is brought into the picture a little bit later, and we will get into that then, but when Messiah first comes into view He comes as a Jew, the *Lion of the Tribe of Judah, the Root of David.* Then He's revealed as the Passover Lamb of Israel. He Himself said: *I wasn't sent to anyone but the lost sheep of the house of Israel.* The apostles said likewise: *God exalted Him with His right hand to be a Prince and a Savior, to give repentance to Israel, and remission of sins. The Lamb* is thus revealed as Israel's Savior and Great Champion. (Mat 15:24, Luk 1:54-55, Act 5:31)

SIT AND WAIT

Notice, now, the position *the Lamb* assumes in Yochanan's description: a *Lamb standing*. From where does He stand? He arises from *the midst of the Throne*. This fulfills prophecy.

Let us turn, now, to a relevant Messianic Psalm. David prophesied regarding the Messiah:

> YHWH says to my Lord, "Sit at My right hand, until I make Your enemies Your footstool for your feet." (Psa 110:1)

Sit at my right hand means "sit next to me on My Throne."

Sit...until means "sit and wait."

Wait *until* what? *Until I make Your enemies Your footstool.*

This terminology places Messiah in Heaven at the *right hand* of YHWH on His Throne. The *footstool* symbolism reinforces that fact, since YHWH says: *Heaven is My Throne, and the earth is My footstool.* This prophecy requires that Messiah must initially *rule in the midst of [His] enemies* from Heaven. All of this is from the Hebrew Scriptures and all of this affirms that Messiah is more than just an ordinary man, even a very good man. According to this Psalm, Messiah must initially rule from Heaven! This agrees with the testimony of Yochanan and all the other early Messianic Jews regarding Y'shua Messiah. They all testify that after overcoming the world, the flesh, and the devil, Messiah overcame death by resurrection from the dead. Then He ascended to Heaven where He *sat down at the right hand of God.* (Psa 110:2, Isa 66:1, Mar 12:36, Luk 20:42, Act 1: 9-11, 2:34, Rom 8:34, Heb 1:3, 8:1, 10:12, 12:2)

STAND, AND STOP WAITING!

Now, let's return to the sitting and standing metaphor. Since *sitting* means waiting, then *standing* means to stop waiting! *Standing,* in this context, is to rise up in Heaven to assume control, while the *enemies* on earth, the *footstool,* are still in power. (Psa 110:1-2)

THE LAMB'S DAY OF POWER

The Psalm continues:

> Your people offer themselves willingly in the day of Your power. (Psa 110:3)

Here, Messiah's *day of power* appears to start with none on earth but His own willing people acknowledging Him, while His enemies are still in power on earth. His *day of power* from Heaven continues progressively from that relatively hidden start. Soon thereafter, all will be forced to recognize His great power. *He will judge among the nations. He will heap up dead bodies. He will crush the ruler of the whole earth.* In other words, the *Lamb standing* to *take the Scroll and to break its seals,* which involves a process of progressive judgment, is equivalent to the standing and progressive judgment by Messiah in Psalm 110. This is the Lamb's Day of Power. (Psa 110:6)

For the most part, Christians know nothing of *the Lamb's Day of Power* involving a progressive judgment on earth originating from Messiah in Heaven–even though it is clearly in view starting with Revelation 5. Generally, they see only His Return as significant. In truth, Messiah will visibly return to complete the Judgment as the grand climax of the Lamb's Day of Power. That blessed event will occur near the end of *the Scroll* that only *the Lamb* is worthy to open, not at the beginning. Until then, Messiah will execute all of the judgments of *the Scroll* from Heaven.

To put this into a time context, The *Day of Judgment* begins when the Heavenly Court is seated in Heaven. *The Lamb's Day of Power* begins shortly thereafter, when the Lamb stands up to take the Scroll from the right hand of the Father, to execute its provisions as the Agent of the Throne. The two time periods start so close to one another, that, in practical terms, they are both the same *Day.* The reference to the Passover Lamb taking the Scroll suggests that *Day* begins on a Passover. This agrees with the claim of the preceding chapter; the Judgment Court of Heaven convened at Passover, 2008.

SYMBOLS OF THE LAMB'S POWER

As we consider the Lamb more closely, as seen in Revelation 5, we have another indication that He is *standing* to exercise power. Look at Him!

> A Lamb...having seven horns, and seven eyes, which are the seven Spirits of God, sent out into all the earth. (Rev 5:6b)

This is no ordinary Lamb. This is a Lamb prepared to exercise power!

Seven horns: Horns are a symbol of power in the Scriptures. As one commentator succinctly points out; "To a pastoral people like the Jews the horns of the strongest in the herd naturally suggested a symbol of power." That being true, this Lamb with *seven horns* definitely is <u>not</u> harmless! In fact, the Lamb having *seven horns* means that He has all power to execute the judgments of the Scroll against His *enemies* on earth. (JFB Commentary on Zec 1:18, see also Psa 89:17, Mic 4:13, Luk 1:69)

Seven eyes: The Lamb sees all by the Holy Spirit. For Him, as for the Father, the seven Spirits are eyes, not merely lamps. The Son is all-knowing, as is His Father. This enables Him to apply His *seven horns of* power to fully execute the judgments of the Scroll. This is yet another reason why He is worthy to take the Scroll and to open its seven seals.

NONE LIKE HIM!

What do you call One who is all-powerful and all-knowing? Call Him: the Divine Son of God! This is why no creature in Heaven or on Earth is worthy to open the Scroll. None are Divine, which is what it takes to accomplish an impossible task. This is why the Son of God emptied Himself to become a man, The Son of Man, to sacrifice Himself for us as the Lamb. No mere creature could have saved us and adopted us into the family of YHWH. None but the perfect Son of God could do that for us! (Psa 110:1, Joh 1:1-5)

PROPHETIC SHORTHAND WEAVES IN ZECHARIAH

There is still more to consider in this manifestation of Y'shua the Messiah, the Lamb, with seven horns and seven eyes. Once again, Revelation is using prophetic shorthand to bring in previous prophecy; in this case, prophecy from Zechariah. As we move forward in Revelation, Zechariah is repeatedly woven into the picture. For that reason, a few basics about Zechariah are now in order.

Zechariah served as prophet during the reign of Darius I of Persia (c. 549 BC–486 BC), whose empire then included the Land of Israel. At that time, a small remnant of Judah had returned from Babylon to Jerusalem. Zechariah's mission to that remnant generation was to give them spiritual encouragement to accomplish the purpose of YHWH; to rebuild the Temple. In the course of that mission, Zechariah also prophesied of the last days, as did all of the prophets.

FOUR HORNS AND FOUR WINDS IN ZECHARIAH

Now, let's consider *horns* in Zechariah.

> I lifted up my eyes, and saw, and behold, four horns. I asked the angel who talked with me, "What are these?" He answered me, "These are the horns which have scattered Judah, Israel, and Jerusalem." (Zec 1:18-19)

We already know that horns symbolize power. Why are there *four horns*? These *four horns* correspond in number to the *four winds* from the four cardinal points of the compass to which the remnant of *Judah, Israel, and Jerusalem* were scattered. Israel scattered to the *four winds* is mentioned by Zechariah a few verses later. The prophetic symbolism is simply this: *four horns* scattered Israel to the *four winds.* (JFB Commentary on Zec 1:18, Zec. 2:6)

What, specifically, are the *four horns* that *scattered Judah, Israel, and Jerusalem* to the *four winds*? The phrase about scattered Israel gives us a clue. Israel, when listed with Judah, refers to the Ten Tribe kingdom of

Israel that was deported from the Land by Assyria well before Zechariah's time. The kingdom of Judah, including Jerusalem, was later deported from the Land by Babylon. Thus, all the Tribes of Israel were deported from the Land by foreign powers. A small remnant returned thereafter from Babylon, to whom Zechariah prophesied. All the rest of Israel, over time, were literally scattered to the *four winds* throughout all the earth.

4 HORNS=4 BEASTS OF DANIEL=GENTILE NATIONS

While it is true that Assyria, and later, Babylon, originally deported all of the tribes of Israel off of the Land, these two empires are not solely responsible for scattering Israel. It took all the Gentile powers of the world, over many generations, to scatter Israel to the *four winds.* These gentile powers are well represented by the four beasts of Daniel, from which they find their origin. In fact, the vision of Daniel regarding the four beasts also connects the four beasts with the *four winds. Daniel spoke and said, I saw in my vision by night, and, behold, the four winds of the sky broke forth on the great sea. Four great animals came up from the sea, diverse one from another.* These four beasts from the *four winds* are further explained by Daniel to be empires that continue in changing form until Judgment Day. The *four horns* of Zechariah are thus revealed to be composed of all the Gentile nations of the earth that have scattered Israel to the *four winds.* (Dan 7, See also Dan 2)

SEVEN TRUMPS FOUR–ISRAEL RE-GATHERED

In Revelation, the Lamb has seven horns, not merely four. The *seven horns* represent more than sufficient power to defeat the *four horns* of the nations that have scattered Israel to the *four winds.* Besides the defeat of the nations, the *seven horns* also suggest the undoing of the scattering of Israel by the *four horns* of the Gentile nations–meaning that the Lamb will re-gather Israel from the *four winds*!

This re-gathering of the remnant of Israel is an important theme of Zechariah, and of Revelation.

SEVEN EYES IN ZECHARIAH

This is underscored as we consider the *seven eyes* which are the *seven Spirits of God.*

> Moreover the word of YHWH came to me, saying, "The hands of Zerubbabel have laid the foundation of this House. His hands shall also finish it; and you will know that YHWH of Hosts has sent me to you. Indeed, who despises the day of small things? For these seven shall rejoice, and shall see the plumb line in the hand of Zerubbabel. These are the eyes of YHWH, which run back and forth through the whole earth." (Zec 4:8-10)

Revelation describes the *seven eyes* as *the seven Spirits of God, sent out into all the earth.* Notice how similar that description is to the phrase, *these seven...the eyes of YHWH, which run back and forth through the whole earth.* The description of the *seven eyes* in Revelation is clearly a paraphrase from this passage in Zechariah. Therefore, to understand the symbolism in Revelation we need to understand it in Zechariah. (Rev 5:6b, Zec 4:8-10)

SEVEN EYES SEE THE TEMPLE OF ZERUBBABEL COMPLETED

As already mentioned, Babylon deported the Kingdom of Judah from the Land. Before doing so Babylon destroyed Jerusalem with Solomon's Temple which was located there. Years later, a remnant of Judah returned with the purpose in mind of rebuilding Jerusalem and the Temple. In the passage above, Zechariah foretells the completed construction of the Second Temple under Governor Zerubbabel. Zerubbabel managed to lay the foundation of the Temple, but then a lengthy period of difficulties ensued in which the surrounding nations, a representative part of the *four horns* above, prevented the completion of the project. Zechariah foretold that by the insight and power of the Holy Spirit, Zerubbabel, who had started the construction of the Temple, would also complete it. In course of time, the prophecy was fulfilled and the Second Temple was, in fact, completed by Governor Zerubbabel.

Let's relate this back to Revelation. Why would Revelation bring in this prophecy about the Temple, which had already been fulfilled in the ancient past? The answer is simple. These words from Zechariah are not only about the Temple of Zerubbabel. These words of Zechariah are also about the last days.

A TYPE OF THE SPIRITUAL TEMPLE

Other commentators on Zechariah have recognized that the construction of the Second Temple was itself a prophecy modeling the coming True Temple in the last days. For example: "Although the words "the hands of Zerubbabel have laid the foundation of this House" unquestionably refer primarily to the building of the earthly temple, and announce the finishing of that building by Zerubbabel, yet the *apodosis* commencing with "and thou shalt know" shows that the sense is not thereby exhausted, but rather that the building is simply mentioned here as a type of the spiritual temple, and that the completion of the typical temple simply furnishes a pledge of the completion of the true temple." (Keil & Delitzsch Commentary on the Old Testament)

There was an actual Temple built by Zerubbabel. However, the prophecy here in Zechariah reaches far beyond that Temple to a "spiritual temple" or "true temple." Just as the Second Temple was completed against all odds by the power of the Holy Spirit, so also will the Spiritual Temple be completed in the last days.

WHAT IS THE SPIRITUAL TEMPLE?

Peter spoke to scattered believing Israelites in the 1st Century, calling them *living stones*, telling them they were being *built up as a Spiritual House,* through Y'shua the Messiah. These were the remnant of Israel in those days that were being built into a Spiritual Temple through Messiah. (1Pe 1:1, 2:5, Rom 11:1-5)

Paul told the Gentile believers of that day that, in joining the remnant of Israel, they were becoming citizens of Israel and part of the True Temple.

He said:

> So then you are no longer strangers and foreigners, but you are fellow citizens with the holy ones (set-apart Israel), and of the household of God, being built on the foundation of the emissaries and prophets, Messiah Y'shua Himself being the chief cornerstone; in whom the whole building, fitted together, grows into a holy Temple in the Lord; in whom you also are built together for a habitation of God in the Spirit. (Eph 2:19-22)

The *foundation* of the True Temple was completed in the 1st Century, and a *building* was begun upon it. However, that construction was later aborted due to oppression by the Gentiles. Actually, an entirely different building was constructed instead. Today we are told that Roman building is the True Temple, but it is not. The True Temple never was of Roman construction. The True Temple must be an Israelite Temple!

UNIQUELY QUALIFIED TO GET THE JOB DONE

The *seven horns* and the *seven eyes* of the Lamb, connecting with all of this from Zechariah, suggests that the time for the re-gathering of the remnant of Israel and the final completion of the Spiritual Temple has come. The message is that the Lamb has the power (*seven horns*) and the knowledge (*seven eyes*) of the Holy Spirit to re-gather Israel and to complete the aborted Spiritual Temple. Nobody other than the Lamb has these qualifications to get these impossible jobs done. He alone *is worthy!*

WHAT THE MAN REVEALS ABOUT THE MISSION

Now, let's relate these Lamb symbols to the contents of the Scroll. The prophetic names and distinguishing features of the One who is worthy to take the Scroll and open it indicate why He is worthy; that is, what His unique qualifications are to open the Scroll. These qualifications are, logically, an indication of what is written in the Scroll itself. On the basis of those qualifications of the Lamb which we have examined to this point, we can be certain Israel is very much at the heart of the Royal Decree.

EARLY INDICATIONS OF THE CONTENTS OF THE SCROLL

Here are some main themes the Lamb's qualifications lead us to expect from the Scroll:

- Israel is about to enter upon her foretold destiny.
- The remnant of Israel will be re-gathered as prophesied.
- The Spiritual Temple will be completed as prophesied.
- The nations that have scattered and oppressed Israel will meet their judgment.

How, exactly, all this will happen remains for the Lamb to reveal after He takes the Scroll out of the right hand of the Father.

HE TOOK THE SCROLL!

> Then He came, and He took it (the Scroll) out of the right hand of Him Who sat on the Throne. (Rev 5:7)

Whereas, all creatures were not worthy to open the Scroll, the Lamb was worthy to step forward to take the Scroll, and to open its seals. He alone has the qualifications needed to do the job. He stood up, and took the Scroll. With that act The Lamb's Day of Power has begun on Judgment Day.

TWO VERSIONS OF WHAT HAPPENED NEXT

Compare these two translations:

> And when he had taken the book, the four beasts and four and twenty elders fell down before the Lamb, having every one of them harps, and golden vials full of odours, which are the prayers of saints. And they sung a new song, saying, Thou art worthy to take the book, and to open the seals thereof: for Thou wast slain, and hast redeemed us to God by thy blood out of every kindred, and tongue, and people, and nation; And hast made us unto our God kings and priests: and we shall reign on the earth. (Rev 5:8-10 KJV)

> When He had taken the book, the four living creatures and the twenty-four elders fell down before the Lamb, each one holding a harp and golden bowls full of incense, which are the prayers of the saints. And they sang a new song, saying, "Worthy are You to take the book and to break its seals; for You were slain, and purchased for God with Your blood men from every tribe and tongue and people and nation. You have made them to be a kingdom and priests to our God; and they will reign upon the earth." (Rev 5:8-10 NASB)

These two translations are typical of the two ways in which these verses are rendered in English translations.

1. The first example presents the beings we have identified as the *four live things* and the *24 Elders* singing a new song in which they say the Lamb has *redeemed us*. This places the *four live things* among the redeemed.

2. The second example presents the beings we have identified as the *four live things* and the *24 Elders* singing a new song in which they say the Lamb has *purchased for God with Your blood men.* This does not place the *four live things* among the redeemed. In other words, as perfect spirit beings, the *four live things* never needed to be redeemed, as do fallen men.

The reason this passage is translated in these two different ways is because there are Greek manuscripts supporting both renderings. The second rendering has the benefit of being harmonious with the surrounding passages while the first rendering does not. The *four live things* and the *24 Elders* are not *out of every kindred, and tongue, and people, and nation* but redeemed *men* are.

THE LIVE THINGS AND THE 24 ELDERS WORSHIP THE LAMB

I am here refining my translation of this passage according to the second, more correct, rendering of the passage. Here is the refined passage:

> Now when He had taken the scroll, the four live things and the twenty-four elders fell down before the Lamb, each one having a harp, and golden bowls full of incense, which are the prayers of the holy ones. They sang a new song, saying, "You are worthy to take the scroll, and to open its seals: for You were killed, and bought for God with Your blood men, out of every tribe, language, people, and nation, and have made them to be a kingdom and priests to our God." (Rev 5:8-10 harmonized with NASB)

Now that we have the correct rendering we return to the flow of the narrative. Participating in the proceedings of the Heavenly Court we have the *four live things,* who are in fact, the *Four Angels of the Presence* around the Throne. We also have the 12 Patriarchs of Israel and the 12 Apostles, making up 24 Elders. These, together, *fell down before the Lamb,* worshiping Him. Clearly, they are not only accepting Him as worthy to take and open the Scroll. More than that, their worship indicates they acknowledge His divine status as Son of God. They each have golden bowls full of *the prayers of the holy ones.* They do not represent themselves only, but also all of the holy ones who have faithfully looked to God in prayer through the generations. It is about those holy ones, whose prayers are answered in the Lamb, that they sing.

A NEW SONG

They sing a *new song.* A *new song* is a new message. Being a song, it's a beautiful message. It's melodious. Let's look now at the substance of the *new song.* They sing; *You were killed, and bought for God with Your blood men, out of every tribe, language, people, and nation.* In Yochanan's day salvation for people of the nations, saved along with believing Israel, was a new mystery revealed. Note that the mystery was never that the Gentiles would replace Israel. Rather, the message was that believing Gentiles could be grafted into Israel to become fellow-citizens with natural Israelite believers. (Rom 11:17, 14:24, Eph 2:11-22, 3:1-7)

Once redeemed by the blood of the Lamb and grafted into believing Israel those Gentile believers participate in the Covenant promise to Israel. This aspect is included in the *new song*: *You have made them to be a kingdom and priests to our God.* They are a *kingdom and priests*, right now.

COVENANT PROMISE TO OBEDIENT ISRAEL

This is a fulfillment of the Covenant promise made to Israel. Let's refresh our memory by quoting that promise here:

> Now therefore, if you will indeed obey My voice, and keep My covenant, then you shall be My own possession from among all peoples; for all the earth is Mine; and you shall be to Me a kingdom of priests, and a holy nation.' These are the words which you shall speak to the children of Israel. (Exo 19:5-6)

By this Covenant promise, obedient Israel was to become *My special possession* and *a Kingdom of priests, and a holy nation.* History shows that much of Israel did not *obey* so did not enter into this Covenant promise. That's why the Prophet Malachi put a finer point on exactly who would enter into the Covenant promise.

A REMNANT AS "MY OWN POSSESSION"

Malachi wrote:

> Then those who feared YHWH spoke one with another; and YHWH listened, and heard, and a book of memory was written before Him, for those who feared YHWH, and who honored His name. "They shall be Mine," says YHWH of Hosts, "My own possession in the Day that I make, and I will spare them, as a man spares his own son who serves him." Then you shall return and discern between the righteous and the wicked, between him who serves God and him who doesn't serve him." (Mal 3:16-18)

Malachi uses the Covenant language of YHWH promising obedient Israel they will be *My own possession.* Malachi does not see this promise applying to all Israelites without distinction. Rather, he foretells a select remnant of Israel to receive the Covenant promise. He makes a distinction between those Israelites who are *righteous* and those who are *wicked.* Only the *righteous* are included. Note also that the promise to the remnant of Israel in Malachi includes the phrase, *you shall return.* This is one of many prophesies foretelling a return of the scattered remnant that YHWH selects to be part of His Covenant nation.

A COVENANT KINGDOM AND PRIESTS

Now, let's notice how Peter the apostle, writing to the scattered remnant of Israel in his day, picks up this same thread.

> But you are a chosen race, a royal priesthood, a holy nation, a people for God's own possession, that you may proclaim the excellence of Him Who called you out of darkness into His marvelous light: who in time past were no people, but now are God's people, who had not obtained mercy, but now have obtained mercy. (1Pe 2:9-10)

Peter saw the Covenant promise to Israel of being a *kingdom and priests* and His *own possession*, being fulfilled in his day upon the faithful remnant of Israel as prophesied by Malachi. This Covenant promise was made to Israel and is fulfilled by the remnant of Israel. Israel was never replaced by some Gentile entity called "The Church." Israel in the Covenant was limited to those Israelites who *obey*, that is, to the faithful remnant of Israel who follow Messiah. To this Israel, Gentile believers are grafted in. Thus, Israel, including grafted in Gentiles, remains at the center of the Royal Decree, at the center of His plan to solve the problem of rebellion. Although this 1st Century picture was aborted by Gentile powers, the Lamb is now getting all of this back on track. (See comments on Rev 1:6 in Chapter 1 of this book. Also, comments on Exo 19:5-6 in Chapter 4 of this book. See also Col 1:13, Exo 19:6, Mal 3:17, 1Pe 2:9)

OUR BLESSED HOPE

They will reign on the earth. The hope of the Elect is not eternity in Heaven. That idea is a Greco-Roman fantasy. Actually, Heaven will be coming here, to the earth, to the Elect, in the form of the New Jerusalem. Revelation here refers to the Hebraic hope of resurrection of the body, which originates in the OT and which was reiterated by Messiah. Our Scriptural hope is to reign on the earth in the Kingdom of Messiah with Him, from the

New Jerusalem in Israel, in a glorified body like His. (Job 19:25-27, Joh 5:28-29, Luk 24:39, 1Jo 3:2-3, Rev 21:3)

WORTHY IS THE LAMB!

The Lamb, having taken the Scroll, and the *four live things* and the 24 *Elders* having sung their *new song*, the scene now changes. We now draw back to take in a wider view:

> And I saw, and I heard something like a voice of many angels around the throne, the live things, and the elders; and the number of them was ten thousands of ten thousands, and thousands of thousands; saying with a loud voice, "Worthy is the Lamb who has been killed to receive the power, wealth, wisdom, strength, honor, glory, and blessing!" (Rev 5:11-12)

We see and hear all the Hosts of Heaven now declaring the Lamb to be worthy!

THE LAMB WILL GET THE JOB DONE!

Next, our vantage point draws back once again, this time, to take in the widest imaginable panorama of both space and time. This scene foresees the end of the Rebellion and the eventual restoration of all creation via the ministry of the Lamb.

> I heard every created thing which is in heaven and on the earth, under the earth and on the sea, and everything in them, saying, "To Him who sits on the throne, and to the Lamb be the blessing, the honor, the glory, and the dominion, forever and ever! Amen!" The four live things said, "Amen!" The elders fell down and worshiped. (Rev 5:13-14)

Amen and amen! There's nothing to cry about. Everything is going to turn out...perfect.

RELEASE OF THE FOUR HORSEMEN

Revelation 6:1-8

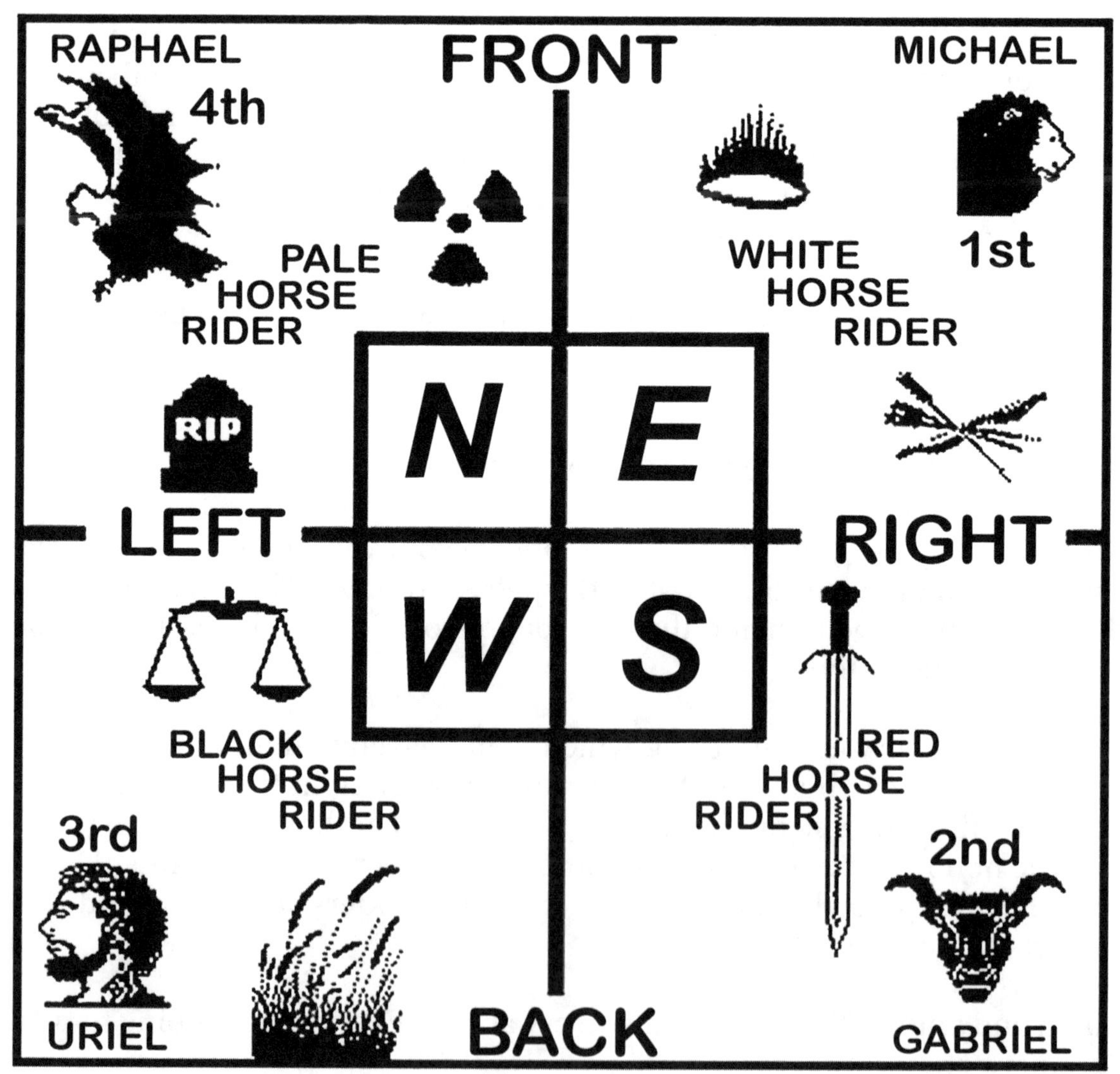

SEALS HAVE BEEN OPENED

Mystery of the Four Horsemen Revealed

The Lamb's Day of Power began in the Heavenly Court early on Judgment Day, when the Lion of the Tribe of Judah stood up and then took the Scroll from the right hand of the Father. Messiah's long wait was over. Quickly, in rapid succession, He removed the first four seals from the Royal Decree. As He opened those first four seals the famous Four Horsemen of Revelation were subsequently released from behind those seals, into the atmosphere of this world. With that decisive release, the judgments made in Heaven are even now making their way into the world of mankind. At Messiah's command, those judgments will continue to be unrolled upon the world, until all that has been written has also been fulfilled.

OPENING OF THE FIRST SEAL

Here, we need to examine this entire scene involving Messiah and the four horsemen to understand its meaning, to comprehend what has now happened. We begin our overview at the opening of the first seal.

> And I saw when the Lamb opened one of the seals, and I heard, as it were the noise of thunder, one of the four live things saying, come and see. (Rev 6:1)

The Lamb standing in the Judgment Court in Heaven opened the first seal and there was a *noise of thunder*. As we have seen earlier, the *noise of thunder* is meant to remind us of Mount Sinai and the covenant YHWH made with Israel. This is an indication that the Covenant with Israel is involved in the opening of this first seal.

The *noise of thunder*, associated with the giving of the Covenant at Sinai, is therefore also a reminder of the annual festival that marks the time that Israel entered into the Covenant at Sinai. That festival is known as Shavuot or Pentecost. This indicates that the first seal was opened on Pentecost, some fifty days after Passover, when Judgment Day began in Heaven.

When the seal was opened "...one of the four live things said 'Come and see.'" The word translated as *one* (G3391 *mia*) can be translated as either *one* or *first*. It should be translated as *first* in this instance, since the passage goes on to list the other live things as *second, third* and *fourth,* as you will soon see.

This is the *first* of the *live things* associated with the *first seal*. Actually, as we will see, each of the *four live things* is associated with its seal and horseman by its corresponding number. Also, each of the *four live things* is also quoted as saying *come and see*. Right now, let's consider what Yochanan saw after the *first seal* was removed.

> "And behold, a white horse, and he who sat on it had a bow. A crown was given to him, and he came forth conquering, and to conquer." (Rev 6:2)

The white horse rider came forth with a *bow* and was given a *crown*. He had been *conquering* and was sent forth to *conquer* some more. The white horse rider is probably the most controversial of all of the riders. An in-depth presentation regarding the white horse rider will be forthcoming later. Right now we want to get the big picture regarding these four horsemen as a whole, which will facilitate our understanding of each one.

OPENING OF THE SECOND SEAL

> "When He opened the second seal, I heard the second live thing saying, "Come!" Another came forth, a red horse. To him who sat on it was given power to take peace from the earth, and that they should kill one another. There was given to him a great sword." (Rev 6:3-4)

We notice the *second seal* was opened. Then the *second live thing* said, *come*. Then the second horse came forth, in this case, a red horse. This horseman was armed with a *great sword* for war. He was given *power to take peace from the earth.*

OPENING OF THE THIRD SEAL

> When He opened the third seal, I heard the third live thing saying, "Come and see!" And behold, a black horse, and he who sat on it had a balance in his hand. I heard a voice in the midst of the four live things saying, "A choenix of wheat for a denarius, and three choenix of barley for a denarius! Don't damage the oil and the wine!" (Rev 6:5-6)

The *third seal* was opened and the *third live thing* was involved here with the third horse. This time it was a black horse. The rider carried a *balance in his hand* and a voice indicated economic woes.

OPENING OF THE FOURTH SEAL

> When He opened the fourth seal, I heard the fourth live thing saying, "Come and see!" And behold, a pale horse, and he who sat on it, his name was Death. Sheol followed with him. Authority over one fourth of the earth, to kill with the sword, with famine, with death, and by the wild animals of the earth was given to him." (Rev 6:7-8)

This is the *fourth seal* and this is the *fourth live thing* that is associated with the fourth horse, the *pale horse*. This rider seems more deadly then all the rest, being named *Death*.

ORIGIN OF FOUR HORSEMEN APOCALYPTIC MOTIF

Now we've taken an initial look at all four horsemen. Their horses are said to be *white*, *red*, *black*, and *pale*. What do these colored horses and their riders really mean? We could just make something up or just guess, as most commentators have done. Many have been fooled by that approach, but real truth-seekers never have been satisfied with such drivel.

To really understand the meaning of these horsemen, we will have to consider them from their source. Contrary to popular belief, these horsemen do not originate in Revelation. Actually, they originate in the writings of the prophet, Zechariah. As we have already learned, he lived some 500 years before the first coming of Messiah. We've already seen that Revelation draws important symbolism from Zechariah. This connection with Zechariah continues as the first four seals are opened.

The prophecy of Zechariah is quite enigmatic for most readers. The Book of Zechariah itself is a "Jewish" apocalyptic book, so it's not comfortable territory for most Christian commentators. Consequently, they generally find it easier to minimize or even leave it out of their teaching on the four horsemen. Here's why you can't minimize or just leave it out: the Four Horsemen Apocalyptic Motif originates in the Book of Zechariah. Revelation is therefore picking up on that apocalyptic literary device and the themes that go with it, drawing them into the Revelation narrative. In other words, comprehending the true meaning of the Four Horsemen of Revelation is impossible if you ignore or minimize reliance upon Zechariah because the Four Horsemen Apocalyptic Motif as used in Zechariah is part of the Revelation story! That means we must at least grasp the essentials of the Four Horsemen Apocalyptic Motif before we can even begin to grasp the meaning of the Four Horsemen of Revelation. Let's read the first three verses of the Book of Zechariah now.

ZECHARIAH PROPHESIED FOR AND TO REMNANT OF ISRAEL

> In the eighth month, in the second year of Darius, the Word of YHWH came to Zechariah, the son of Berechiah, the son of Iddo the prophet, saying, "YHWH was very displeased with your fathers. Therefore tell them: Thus says YHWH of Hosts: 'turn back to me,' says YHWH of Hosts, 'and I will turn back to you,' says YHWH of Hosts." (Zec 1:1-3)

These verses establish the context in which the whole Book of Zechariah was written. We notice the ministry of Zechariah commenced in the second year of Darius. Darius was the King of Persia. Persia had conquered Babylon. Earlier, Babylon had been the instrument that YHWH had used to punish the Kingdom of Judah. All of the Judeans of any importance had been deported off of the Land to Babylon, where they had remained in captivity for most of a generation. That's what the verse means when it says, "*YHWH was very displeased with your fathers.*" He brought severe punishment upon that earlier generation including the destruction of the city of Jerusalem and the Temple, and the deportation of the people from the Land. YHWH had been angry with them for a lot of very good reasons.

In Zechariah's time, those circumstances had changed. The Persians were now in control and they were of a mind to release the Judeans to return to the Land. A faithful remnant did return to the Land from Babylon, with the task of rebuilding the Temple. YHWH sent Zechariah to that remnant with a message: *Turn back to Me, says YHWH of Hosts, and I will turn back to you, says YHWH of Hosts.* The Book of Zechariah is therefore about turning back, about repentance of a faithful remnant of Israel.

Be aware that not all who had been deported to Babylon, or who had been born in captivity there, chose to return to Israel to accomplish the Divine Will. Actually, most chose to stay in Babylon rather than brave the challenges involved in returning to the Land. The Book of Zechariah is not about those shirkers who stayed in Babylon. Rather, it is about the earnest remnant of overcomers who turned back to YHWH and went on to get the job done. This involved returning back to the Land, making a home there, and re-building the Temple of YHWH in Jerusalem.

It is not surprising that the apocalyptic book of Zechariah, while being immediately concerned with the remnant of Israel of his day, speaks also to the remnant of Israel in the last days. The Book of Revelation frequently refers back to Zechariah because Zechariah is talking about important themes shared with Revelation. Since the Book of Zechariah is primarily about the remnant of Israel and what they did in turning back to YHWH, Revelation is about the remnant of Israel too. Indeed, a primary point of convergence between Revelation and Zechariah is that they are both written for, to, and about the faithful remnant of Israel. The end goal for the remnant of Israel in each book is the rebuilding of the Temple. That is a key point to remember as we consider the horsemen.

FOUR HORSEMEN OF ZECHARIAH

Now that we understand that Zechariah is to, for, and about the faithful remnant of Israel, let's specifically consider the horses. What are these colored horses about? We find them in the very first chapter of Zechariah, directly connected with the remnant and the return of the remnant to Israel. Zechariah reports his vision.

> I had a vision in the night, and behold, a man riding on a red horse, and he stood among the myrtle trees that were in a ravine; and behind him there were red, brown, and white horses. Then I asked, 'My lord, what are these?'"
>
> The angel who talked with me said to me, "I will show you what these are."
>
> The man who stood among the myrtle trees answered, "They are the ones YHWH has sent to go back and forth through the earth."
>
> They reported to the angel of YHWH who stood among the myrtle trees, and said, "We have walked back and forth through the earth, and behold, all the earth is at rest and in peace." (Zec 1:8-11)

There are both similarities and dissimilarities between this vision and the Revelation vision of the horses. Similarities include the number of horses, namely four. The four horses varied from one another in color in both visions. The horsemen in both visions are sent forth from YHWH and answer to angels. These strong points of congruence are sufficiently meaningful to establish that the four horsemen of Zechariah are the source of the concept of the four horsemen in Revelation. The dissimilarities will aid our understanding after we bring in more information, a bit farther along.

THE REPORT OF THE HORSEMEN TO THE ANGEL

Let's now focus on the report given by the horsemen to the angel. They said; *we have walked back and forth through the earth, and behold, all the earth is at rest and in peace.*

Peace in all the earth is a good thing, right? Wrong. Not this time anyway. This is seen by the angel's reply to YHWH due to the report from the horsemen of *rest* and *peace* in *all the earth.*

> Then the angel of YHWH replied, "O YHWH of Hosts, how long will you not have mercy on Jerusalem and on the cities of Judah, against which you have had indignation these seventy years?" (Zec 1:12)

Notice that the angel interpreted peace in the earth among the nations as being a continuation of the seventy year *indignation* of YHWH against Israel. The angel, (whom I believe to be Michael, advocate of Israel) implores YHWH on behalf of Israel.

THE RESPONSE OF YHWH TO THE REPORT OF THE HORSEMEN

YHWH responds to the report of the horsemen and the angel's reply.

> "**I am jealous for Jerusalem and for Tsiyon** with a great jealousy. **I am very angry with the nations that are at ease**; for I was but a little displeased, but they added to the calamity."
>
> Therefore thus says YHWH: "I have returned to Jerusalem with mercy. **My House shall be built** in it," says YHWH of Hosts, "and a line shall be stretched forth over Jerusalem."'
>
> "Proclaim further, saying, 'Thus says YHWH of Hosts: "My cities will again overflow with prosperity, and **YHWH will again comfort Tsiyon**, and will again choose Jerusalem." (Zec 1:15-17)

THE FOUR HORSEMEN OF ZECHARIAH RIDE FOR ISRAEL

This puts the four horsemen of Zechariah in perspective. They were sent out to observe what was happening in the earth **in relation to Israel** and to report back to the angel. When the angel received the report that the nations were *at rest* he became concerned for Israel, and cried out to YHWH. The *rest* and *peace* of the nations is at Israel's expense! Enough of that! YHWH became angry at the nations at rest, vowing that the Temple would be rebuilt, that mercy would flow to Jerusalem and that prosperity would be returned to the cities of the Land. *YHWH will again comfort Tsiyon* He says.

From here it is very tempting to launch into the Four Horsemen of Revelation. However, we must be patient, because we have another passage in Zechariah we must bring into our field of view. We have riders again in Zechariah chapter six.

FOUR CHARIOTEERS OF ZECHARIAH RIDE THE FOUR WINDS

> Again I lifted up my eyes, and saw, and behold, four chariots came out from between two mountains; and the mountains were mountains of brass.
>
> With the first chariot were red horses; with the second chariot black horses;
>
> With the third chariot white horses; and with the fourth chariot dappled horses, all of them powerful.
>
> Then I asked the angel who talked with me, "What are these, my lord?"
>
> The angel answered me, "These are the four winds of the sky, which go forth from standing before the Lord of all the earth. (Zec 6:1-5)

Here we have a variation on the Four Horsemen Apocalyptic Motif, with four charioteers this time. Again we have both similarities and dissimilarities between this vision and the Revelation horsemen vision, as well as with the horsemen vision of Zechariah chapter one. Similarities again include horses of varied colors in each of the three visions. The colors of these horses in Zechariah six seem to be very similar to the colors of the horses of Revelation. Again there are four riders. Also, the Source of the horses in all three cases is YHWH. As Zechariah chapter six continues, we find the theme of the return of the remnant and the rebuilding of the Temple still in view. The last verse of Zechariah chapter six summarizes; *those who are far off shall come and build in the Temple of YHWH.* This remnant of Israel theme is essential to the Four Horsemen Apocalyptic Motif in both Zechariah visions. This remnant of Israel theme must therefore be carried forward with the Four Horsemen Motif as applied in Revelation. (Zec 6:15)

THREE SEPARATE MISSIONS

Now, let's consider dissimilarities. Here we have four charioteers rather than four horsemen. While the colors of the chariot horses are very similar to the horses of Revelation, the horses of Zechariah chapter one vary significantly from the other two horsemen visions. Why the dissimilarities?

Simply put, each vision is of a different mission than the other two. That's why in each case the horses chosen for the given mission vary, as do the presence or absence of chariots or other equipage. Also, the varying relative destinations in each case speak of a unique mission from the other two, as do the time differences for each mission.

RIDERS OF THE FOUR WINDS

Zechariah six brings in some important new information illuminating this symbolism. Here the angel associates the horses with *the four winds of the sky which go forth from standing before the Lord of all the earth.*

In ancient Hebraic thought, the four winds of the cardinal points of the earth go forth from the Throne of YHWH in Heaven. This is a symbolic picture of the Heavenly "on-ramp" by which YHWH releases the agents of His influence from Heaven (represented as riders) into the four winds blowing throughout the earth, to accomplish their given mission among the nations of mankind.

Imagine this picture: YHWH is in Heaven, sitting upon His Throne in the manner we've already discussed in earlier chapters. The four winds of the earth issue forth from beneath His Throne platform in Heaven to the east, south, west and north, from whence they make their way into a wind-highway system extending into every corner of the earth. At the Divine command, four riders are sent out on the four winds to carry His influence into the earth, to accomplish the specific mission for which they are sent.

FOUR ARCHANGELS SEND FOUR RIDERS INTO FOUR WINDS

While each given mission is conceived and initiated by YHWH, He does not Personally dispatch the riders into the winds. Here in Zechariah, we notice that there are angels associated with the four riders, just as in Revelation. They are the four Archangels who are stationed around the Throne of YHWH, constantly standing in His presence, one at each of the four points of the compass, each directly over their corresponding wind. It is each of these four angels who actually send each of the riders into each of the four winds, following upon their Divine release. That's what has taken place in Zechariah and in the Book of Revelation regarding the four horsemen, in each of the three respective missions reported. I have found that other Hebraic apocalyptic literature also agrees with this picture.

UNLOCKING THE MYSTERY OF THE 4 RIDERS OF REVELATION

Needless to say, this insight is a key that can unlock the true meaning of the Four Horsemen of Revelation to us. Let's go back to the description of what happens at the opening of the first four seals in Revelation, applying this knowledge to that description.

In our initial examination of Revelation 6:1-8 we observed what happened as Messiah unsealed each of the first four seals. We noted that each of the *four live things* was associated by its number to its corresponding seal and horseman. Each of the *four live things* is quoted as saying "Come and see"—apparently speaking to Yochanan. This is misleading. A majority of manuscripts indicate the live things did not say "Come and see." A Christian commentary explains; "One oldest manuscript, B, has "And see." But A, C, and *Vulgate* reject it. Alford rightly objects to *English Version* reading: "Whither was John to come? Separated as he was by the glassy sea from the throne, was he to cross it?" (Jamieson, Fausset and Brown Commentary, Rev 6:1)

The live things did not say "Come and see." A majority of manuscripts indicate they each simply said "*Come*." They were not speaking to Yochanan. Rather, they were each speaking to their respective horseman released when unsealed by Messiah, commanding that horseman to *come*; to enter the wind over which the respective live thing exercised control. Further, this occurred in rapid succession moving to each cardinal position around the Throne, so that each of the four horsemen went out upon its appointed wind at about the same time as the others. As in Zechariah, the riders are sent out on the four winds in sets of four at a time.

SIGNIFICANCE OF VARIED MISSIONS

In Zechariah, we observed two missions in which riders were sent out into the four winds. Both of those missions were merely reconnaissance missions in which the riders observed what was going on in the earth relative to the remnant of Israel, and then reported back. This is why the riders of Zechariah are not seen to be carrying weapons or other gear. They were not sent out to actually change anything in the world of mankind, but only to observe and then make a report. They needed no weapons or equipment to do that. By contrast, the Four Horsemen of Revelation are given weapons and other equipment for use in their mission. Why? Because Judgment Day has come! The Four Horsemen of Revelation are, in fact, the first tangible agents of Judgment Day sent forth by Messiah specifically for the purpose of unleashing His righteous judgments upon the world of mankind. This time they are not only observing on behalf of the remnant of Israel—now, they are released to inflict the introductory judgments of the Scroll upon the world for Israel's sake!

By examining the details regarding each of the Four Horsemen of Revelation, and the Archangel that released each one, we can comprehend the scope of the judgment Messiah has released into the world through the horsemen in these introductory judgments of Judgment Day. These judgments are to be manifested in specific events, each in their appointed time.

THE FIRST SEAL REVEALED

The first seal is the most important because it not only sealed its respective section of the Scroll, but even more importantly, it sealed the Scroll in its entirety. Once the first seal was broken the judgment had begun, and nothing in Heaven above or earth underneath can stop the flow of predetermined judgment events that must be completely exhausted in due order from the time of that breaking of the first seal, unto the end of the age.

Be aware that I am <u>not</u> saying the Great Tribulation started at the breaking of the first seal. According to the prophetic schedule much must occur first, during this preliminary judgment period, before the appointed time for the Great Tribulation will arrive. The Four Horsemen of Revelation are the agents of the introductory judgments that will prepare the ground for later judgment events. Time must be allowed for the horsemen to do their work.

Now, here is the refined translation regarding the opening of the first seal.

> And I saw when the Lamb opened the first of the seven seals, and I heard, as it were the noise of thunder (and) the first of the four live things saying, "Come." And I saw and behold, a white horse, and he that sat on him had a bow. And a crown was given to him, and he went forth conquering, and to conquer. (Rev 6:1-2)

The first of the four live things is the archangel, Michael. Michael is the first and greatest of the archangels. He is the chief prince among the archangels. He is the leader of all of the Hosts of Heaven and the Scriptures tell us he will *stand up* for Israel in the Great Tribulation. Through the Tribulation, Michael, and therefore, all of the Heavenly Host under His command, will be standing on behalf of the remnant of Israel. That's an encouraging thought, isn't it? Michael is historically the protector of Israel. Jewish apocalyptic sources present Michael as helping Israel in numerous ways from Abraham forward. He's also shown as opening the gates of justice for the righteous. He blows the last trump in the Jewish literature. In the Book of Enoch, he's associated with forbearance and mercy and he's called the *prince of Israel.* Artistically, he's depicted in white armor.

Michael is located among the *four live things* stationed around the Throne. Being the foremost of the four, he's in the right front position on the Throne platform, the *first* position among the four. Biblically, right is the side of greatest favor and the right front position is the place of leadership among the Heavenly Hosts. As we've mentioned Michael is the advocate for Israel and Israel is also, in a symbolic sense, in that same right front position. This corresponds to the east in Scripture. Finally, we remember that Michael is the live thing with an appearance like a lion.

The white horse rider, the first horseman, was called forth by Michael when the first seal was broken. White is the color of righteousness and justice, for which Michael stands. This fact is at odds with most interpreters of the four horsemen. The tendency is to make the white horse rider a "bad guy" since the other three horsemen appear to be "bad guys." For this reason the most popular interpretation is that the white horse rider is the anti-Christ or pictures the anti-Christ spirit coming into the world. This theory flies in the face of the fact that in the Book of Revelation, in every instance white is associated with righteousness, justice and holiness. Further, Revelation presents the anti-Christ as coming forth from the devil, not from Michael the Archangel. Clearly, the stance that the white horse rider is the anti-Christ, or other evil figure, is a guess arising from ignorance of what is really going on in the Revelation narrative.

Since we are saying that the white horse rider is not a "bad guy" then we must also explain why he alone is not a "bad guy" when the other three horsemen clearly appear to be so. Armed with the clarity of this Revelation scene now revealed, that becomes crystal clear. Very simply, Michael is advocate for Israel, so we would expect that this particular horse is associated with Israel also. Michael is located on the east, so released the white horse rider into the east wind. The white horse rider was actually released towards the remnant of Israel, prophetically located on the east. The first judgment of the Scroll is a blessing for Israel.

Remember, Messiah is acting as Champion of Israel. Therefore, the white horse rider is primarily sent to benefit Israel, Messiah's first concern. He's being sent on the right hand of the favor of God! Who exactly is he? The answer to that question merits a book of its own in this series. For now, suffice it to say that he is a messenger sent forth from Messiah to provide the remnant of Israel what they need to meet the challenges of Judgment Day. He is armed (the bow) and authorized (the crown) for exactly that purpose. The primary mission of the remnant of Israel, as indicated in Zechariah, is the completion of the Temple—in this case the Spiritual Temple as mentioned in chapter six of this book. We would expect the white horse rider to be facilitating that mission.

Unlike the white horse rider, the other three horsemen are all sent as judgment upon the nations of the earth that are complicit in scattering and oppressing Israel through these many generations. That is why those three riders represent punishing judgments while the white horse rider does not. From the standpoint of those Gentile nations, those other three horsemen are definitely perceived as "bad guys" bringing troubles upon them. From the perspective of the Gentile nations that hate Israel, the white horse rider, riding for Israel, is considered a "bad guy" too–though the righteous of all nations will not see it that way.

THE SECOND SEAL REVEALED

Now, here is the refined translation regarding the opening of the second seal.

> And when He opened the second seal, I heard the second live thing saying, "Come!" And another horse went out, red. And it was given to the one sitting on it to take peace from the earth, and that they should slay one another. And a great sword was given to him. (Rev 6:3-4)

The second live thing is the archangel, Gabriel, the Messenger of God. We know some things about Gabriel from the Scriptures. He is most remembered for being sent to announce Messiah's birth to Mary. In the Book of Daniel, chapter eight, we find him acting as a messenger of the end times. In other Jewish apocalyptic literature, Gabriel is regarded as the angel of death who struck down the firstborn of the Egyptians. Gabriel is also credited with destroying the armies of Sennacherib. That involved 185,000 enemy troops slain by the angel in one night! Sanhedrin 95b says Gabriel was armed "with a sharpened scythe which has been ready since creation" for that chore. Gabriel is shown in Revelation with the appearance of a young bull, signifying the tremendous power resident within one capable of such prodigious acts of warfare as these. (2Ki 19:35, Isa 37:36)

The red horse rider is well-paired with the archangel, Gabriel. Bulls are often red even as this horse is red—even as blood is red. More importantly, this horseman is sent forth to instigate war, *that they should slay one another*. Many of Sennacherib's troops were slain in exactly this same way, slaying one another. Gabriel was said to be armed with *a sharp scythe*, while the rider of the red horse was given *a great sword*. In both cases the prepared weapon produces the same result: death by warfare on a massive scale. This is part of the judgment that Messiah has sent forth into the world to be manifested in His appointed times.

CHECKING THE COMPASS IN HEAVEN

Perhaps as we have begun to proceed around the Throne, you have noticed that the points of the compass are not aligned there the way you might expect. In our modern thinking, we always put north first. This is not so in this scene. Biblically, each of the points of the compass has a different meaning. East is the most favored point on the compass, being associated with Israel, on God's right hand. Therefore, as we've seen, east is the location of the first and the foremost of the four winds, and the first and the foremost of the Archangels.

Next, moving compass-wise, we come to the right rear position. Still being right of the Throne, this remains the most favored side, though; being in the rear it is not the lead position. On the compass, this is south. This is the location of the *second live thing*, the archangel, Gabriel. Biblically the south is often associated with Egypt and everything that Egypt represents. Often, Egypt signifies the unredeemed world generally. The red horse rider, released into the south wind, removes peace from the earth generally, rather than being focused on a particular location.

Next, we move to the left rear position in relation to the Throne. On the compass, this is west. This is the position demanding our attention as the *third seal* is opened.

THE THIRD SEAL REVEALED

> When he opened the third seal, I heard the third live thing saying, "Come!" And behold, a black horse, and he who sat on it had a balance in his hand. I heard a voice in the midst of the four live things saying, "A choenix of wheat for a denarius, and three choenix of barley for a denarius! Don't damage the oil and the wine!" (Rev 6:5-6)

The third live thing is the archangel, Uriel. Uriel is listed as the third angel in the Testament of Solomon and also in the Book of Esdras, so he fits very well in this third position. Uriel means "Fire of God." He also is called by the name Phenuel meaning "Face of God." Revelation presents the third live thing with the appearance of a man. Man was created in God's image, so "Face of God" is a fitting name. Uriel is known as the angel of repentance. His name, "Fire of God," likely relates to the refining fire of trials that produce repentance.

Enter the black horse rider. In the Scriptures, God often uses want to turn people to repentance. The scales in his hand and the talk of goods and money demonstrate that the black horse rider is harbinger of a global economic crisis resulting in severe shortages and even famine. A *choenix* is about a quart and a *denarius* is about a day's wage for the working man in Bible times. The cry going forth with this rider declares a quart of wheat costs a day's wage. This might be enough wheat to make a small loaf of bread.

Can you imagine working all day to buy barely enough to feed one man, let alone your whole family? Many people in the world are there already. On the other hand *the oil and the wine* are untouched by the crisis. Oil and wine are associated with the rich. The picture here is clear. While the wage earner is literally being starved, the rich aren't being hurt at all. This seems to suggest that the crisis likely originates with the wealthy. Along this vein, we should also note that the black horse goes out on the west wind. The economic crisis originates in the west, in America, and affects the whole world from there. Have you seen that black horse in your neighborhood lately? If so, then take it as the kindness of God, as He sends the economic crisis as a refining fire in the hearts of men, to turn them to God before time for repentance has run out. (Hos 11:10)

THE FOURTH SEAL REVEALED

> When he opened the fourth seal, I heard the fourth live thing saying, "Come!" And behold, a pale horse, and he who sat on it, his name was Death. Sheol followed with him. Authority over one fourth of the earth, to kill with the sword, with famine, with death, and by the wild animals of the earth was given to him. (Rev 6:7-8)

The fourth live thing is the archangel, Raphael. His name means "God heals." Interestingly, he is associated with yellow and green in Jewish apocalyptic literature. Raphael has the appearance of an eagle in Revelation.

In the Book of Enoch, Raphael became arch-enemy of azazel, a particularly diabolical leader of the angels that sinned by fornication with daughters of men, arguably second only to the devil in the dark ranks of wickedness and power. azazel compounded his sins by revealing secrets of technology to mankind that they were not prepared to know. These included the working of metals to create deadly weapons of war as well as the making of the first alluring apparel, jewelry and cosmetics. Apparently, like other pimps and pushers of all stripes, azazel supplied evil goodies to everybody–for a price. Predictably, the illicit release of this forbidden technology led to mass violence and corruption in the earth. azazel had to be stopped. YHWH sent Raphael to bind azazel and seal him up in a great abyss until the final judgment, wherein certain doom awaits. Raphael speedily put away this angelic bad boy, azazel, whose name means something like "rough and mighty." In this exploit, Raphael demonstrated himself to be more than a match for any nasty spirit out there, no matter how evil, bloodthirsty, or powerful. (1 Enoch 8:1-3a, 10:4-6)

Raphael is stationed at the left-front position in relation to the Throne, over the north wind. From ancient times the enemies of Israel tend to come down against Israel from the north, even if originating elsewhere. This continues to be true today. For example, Iran is not located north of Israel and yet, Iran sends its client-terrorists and attackers from the north. In Scripture, the north is therefore associated with the enemies of Israel. The north is at the immediate left hand of the Throne, showing the disdain of YHWH towards the enemies of Israel.

How did the left hand come to be regarded in this way? Forgive me if this is a bit course, but it is the real answer. Biblical cultures from antiquity have generally reserved the left hand for care of bodily functions, while the right hand is assigned more honorable use. To offer your left hand to someone in that culture is to say you regard them as...well, something less than honorable. The left hand is therefore the place of the least favor or even of disdain. This does not indicate that the angel Raphael, stationed at the left of the Throne, is held in disdain. Rather, he is stationed in that place like an eagle; watching and poised to speedily swoop down upon those enemies of YHWH who <u>are</u> held in disdain by the Throne, as in the case of azazel related above.

The pale horse rider is the horseman released into the north wind by the *fourth live thing*, Raphael. This rider has a name: Death. Sheol (the grave) is riding with him, ready to swallow up the many victims wherever this horseman rides. The color of his horse gives us some idea of why this rider is so deadly. While it is here translated as *pale* the color is actually translated from the Greek word *chloros,* related to our English word, *chlorophyll.* It is a pale shade of green, greenish-yellow specifically. In the atomic age this is the color associated with radiation, with atomic war. (Robertson's Word Pictures, Rev 6:8)

Authority over one fourth of the earth, to kill with the sword, with famine, with death, and by the wild animals of the earth was given to him. Unlike the red horse rider, who only kills with the sword, this rider has multiple means to destroy large numbers of people rapidly and thoroughly. Since he is released toward the north, his target has to be the enemies of Israel. Indeed, he is not sent into all the earth but is limited in authority to *one fourth of the earth.* How amazing that Islam, the main aggressor against Israel today, comprises about *one fourth* of the earth's population!

Bloodthirsty Islam is fueled by a crazed spirit who seeks world domination. In reality allah is a minor fallen spirit who once feigned to be the desert moon god. Motivated by delusions of grandeur, he has since gone on to attempt to usurp the place of the God of Israel, even as his worshippers have attempted to usurp the place of Israel for themselves. As Raphael swooped down upon the presumptuous azazel to swiftly remove him from influence, so also will the presumptuous allah soon meet a similar fate, with a swiftness that will shock the world. This will take the form of the fourth horseman bringing swift and massive death upon those Islamic enemies of Israel who, right now, are plotting her doom. The disaster they scheme against Israel is about to fall upon their own heads with stunningly horrible effect. This massive defeat of Israel's enemies will mean doom to them, but healing for Israel, thus the name Raphael, "God heals."

Tragically, millions will die in the judgment against the anti-Israel coalition of nations that are gathered under the umbrella of Islam. Please, so long as there is yet time; pray for the deliverance of the righteous who now live in Islamic lands!

IT'S ABOUT ISRAEL—AND YOU

This picture becomes clearer, the more we look at it. Let's re-cap. On the front right hand, the east, we have Israel in the place of Divine favor. First among all the horses, and all the seals, the white horse rider is released by Messiah, the Champion of Israel. He is then sent out on the east wind to the remnant of Israel by Michael, advocate for Israel. This reflects the Scriptural fact that Israel is of first concern among the nations.

Next, we have two horsemen sent out to the nations of the world. Their mission involves inflicting judgments upon those Gentile nations who have scattered and oppressed Israel generally, through the generations. While punishing judgments upon the world are involved here, the hope of repentance for all who will respond is also very much in view.

The fourth horseman named *Death* is by far the most terrible. Right now he is riding the north wind, maneuvering and shaping geopolitical forces to allow an Islamic coalition of enemy nations of Israel to formulate the hatred that is already in their hearts into an evil scheme against Israel. These nations will be emboldened, at the appointed time, to threaten the very existence of the nation of Israel. When this scheme has sufficiently ripened, the black horse rider will inflict severe judgments of death upon those Islamic enemy nations. Indications are this will involve an atomic war that will bring instant devastation and death upon those nations plotting the demise of Israel, but before they can launch the same upon Israel. Their evil plot will be turned around upon their own heads. This judgment will fall so rapidly, and will inflict such massive death, that it will completely stun the rest of the inhabitants of planet earth and will completely change the geo-political balance of the world in Israel's favor. This will prepare the way for the faithful remnant of the Twelve Tribes of Israel to go home to the Land in a second exodus. (Psa 83, Isa 11:10-16, 17:1, Mic 7:15-20, Zec 10:6-12)

Informed by themes from Zechariah woven into Revelation, what we are seeing here is the beginning of the appointed time period foretold by all the prophets when YHWH returns His favor to scattered Israel. Zechariah spoke primarily for and to the remnant of Israel, but he also spoke of things having to do with the Land of Israel. Likewise, by *Israel* I mean the Land of Israel, which can include Abraham's seed residing there, and I mean the faithful remnant of the Twelve Tribes of Israel that have been scattered throughout the earth. All the prophets foretold a time of favor for scattered Israel in the last days in which YHWH will regather Israel and restore them to His Land for His glory. All of the righteous of every nation are called to abandon the failed religious system, falling Babylon, to align themselves with Israel's Messiah, and with His believing remnant of Israel. All persons who do not do so will end up aligned with the enemies of YHWH and will share in their judgment. (Hag 2:5-9, Mic 4:10-13, Zec 2, Rev 18:4)

WHAT WE CAN EXPECT FROM THE FOUR HORSEMEN

Future volumes will examine the individual horsemen in much more depth. Our purpose in this chapter has been to present an overview of the meaning of the Four Horsemen of Revelation, to provide insight into how they fit into the picture already revealed of Judgment Day. Here we will share a few thoughts putting all this in practical context, to get an overall concept of what we can expect during the ride of the horsemen.

Realize that, while the horsemen each have a unique mission of their own, they are sent out and operate during the same time period, delivering early judgments upon the world. Thus, the events associated with each of the horsemen interact in a complex way. For example, global economic crisis (black horse) likely contributes to war (red horse) and visa versa. Likewise, both of those could easily help set the stage for the pale horse events to occur and visa versa. Meanwhile, the white horse rider performs his mission on behalf of Israel throughout all of those events. The end result of this complex interaction between the four horsemen appears to onlookers as world events spiraling out of control. Periods of relative calm will give way to waves of global disaster, seemingly without warning. These waves will increase in both frequency and intensity over time, as with the pains of a woman in travail. (Mat 24:6-8)

As those judgment peaks get ever more severe so will the sense of alarm built up by them. Many will believe that the Great Tribulation is here, when in fact this travail will go on without end longer than nominal believers are prepared to tolerate. Millions will become bitter because they have not been "raptured out" of the world's increasing troubles. As a result, many who are now perceived as believers will succumb to unbelief and will even become bitter enemies against the Kingdom. I am telling you this now so that you do not grow weary in your faith; that you may endure to the end. Judgment Day is here. The Great Tribulation is not here and will not be here for a pre-determined period of years. First, the events of the four horsemen must do their work of separating many of the wicked from the righteous in preparation for the final decisive events of the Great Tribulation. (Dan 11:35, Mal 4:1, Hab 2:3, Mat 24:13, 45-51 Luk 21:12-19)

THE ENDING POINT—THE STARTING POINT

You have now nearly finished reading this book. All that is left is this paragraph and a little bit in the *Epilogue* to tie up a few loose ends. It is time to start thinking about what this book, taken as a whole, means to your life.

Perhaps you have perceived that this first volume in this *Messianic Revelation Series* is not primarily about the future. It is primarily about the present, relative to the prophesied events of Revelation. This book is therefore an announcement of present heavenly realities that affect everyone, whether they know of these realities or not. You have the advantage of having this book in your hand. I don't believe in coincidences, do you? I think there is a reason this information found its way to you. Only you and God can determine what that reason is, but it surely has to do with your place in the plan of YHWH. The information in this book is meant to be a starting point, as you make your way through Judgment Day unto the end. Please accept this message as His call to examine your beliefs, your life and your relationship to Him, to prepare yourself for momentous events already scheduled at specific points in the remainder of this last generation, here, at the end of the age.

Also, consider this: now you know things that very few people are aware of regarding the times we live in. You will need to decide what you will do with this information. Who will you share it with? How will you share it? Everything is different now. Get with God, in earnest prayer, and search out what all of this means for you. (Eze 3:17-21, Jam 1:22-25, 4:7-10, 5:7-11, 5:16-20)

EPILOGUE

Reading this section before finishing the book would be like watching the special features on a DVD before finishing the movie. Most people don't do that because, without having seen the movie the special features don't make sense, or worse, spoil the movie. This section is like the special features section on a DVD, in that, it is meant to answer questions left when the "movie" is over. That's why, If you haven't finished the rest of this book already, I would encourage you to do so now, before reading this section. Oh, one more thing. Please don't reveal details from this section to others until after they have read the book too. (Don't you just hate it when someone reveals the end of a story before you get there yourself?)

Past this page I'm writing assuming you've read everything to this point. After reading this book certain questions have undoubtedly surfaced in your mind. I hope to answer some of those questions here. Others will likely be answered by the remaining volumes in this series. Why so many questions?

Very often a book will be written about one new idea. This book presents many ideas that are new to readers. Dealing with so many new ideas from one book can be a strain, especially if those ideas do not fit into one's pre-existing paradigm. Realize that this book is less then one seventh of the whole message, so there is much more to come before the whole picture is complete. Even so, what I have presented in this book, and will be presenting in future volumes, form into one harmonious whole that breaks the barrier of superficiality. This is in-depth truth in plain language that aligns with known facts, forming into a comprehensive and cohesive big picture, shattering all previous interpretations of Revelation.

If you comprehend the significance of this presentation to this point, your first question is probably: "how did you (the author) come to know all this?" Following is the real answer to that question.

If I told you that I have been diligently studying the Scriptures from the time I was a child; that would be true. If I said that I am a dedicated Scripture researcher who has learned to ferret out the facts through long years of experience; that also would be true. If I told you I have been in the ministry for nearly three decades; that would be true as well. Indeed, all of these factors played some role in this book.

None of these factors, however, can explain how I have been able to describe a scene in Heaven in striking detail – a scene that, until now, the greatest scholars and doctors of theology from all the seminaries and Bible colleges of the world have neither been able to accurately comprehend nor explain. Am I really saying that I am smarter than ALL of them? If I made that claim would you believe me? I didn't think so.

No, I'm not that smart. My answer to you has to be the same answer that Daniel offered to king Nebuchadnezzar when Daniel revealed things that were beyond the mind of man to know. "There is a God in heaven who reveals secrets, and he has made known ... what shall be in the latter days." Yes, YHWH deserves the credit for this hidden knowledge, not me, nor any man. True to form in this book, I will go beyond merely stating the obvious fact that Divine secrets originate from Heaven, to give you an account of exactly when and how YHWH revealed to me this knowledge, this news, written in this book. (Dan 2:28)

At Passover of 2008 this Revelation message began to come to me in the Spirit like a flood. At that time there were two other adults living in my home. The first I will mention is Dawn, my beloved life and ministry partner, who then and now was hard at work being a mom, home schooling and caring for our five children. I say "ministry partner" because, in addition to her family role, Dawn is also a vital part of the Tsiyon ministry in more ways than I can tell you here. For example, she laid out this entire book for publication, as she does all of my books. In a very real way, Dawn and I function as a unit. Dawn brings unique qualities, talents and abilities to the ministry that greatly enable the message, and her role in helping to bring this book to you is no exception to that. Here, as you read on, Dawn offers her account of what occurred as I was receiving this Revelation message.

Before you hear from Dawn, though, I want to tell you about the other person who was living with us at that time. SueJean, an American missionary to Asia, had responded to our radio messages by becoming a Tsiyon Radio volunteer. Among other things, she does transcription and editing of our Tsiyon materials, including radio program messages that subsequently became encapsulated in this book. She also did a great job trolling for typos in my manuscript (thank you SueJean, for your help!). Just a couple weeks before Passover of 2008 she came to live with our family at our home to lend a helping hand for a while, and remained through most of that year. As it turns out, Sue Jean is also a world class prayer warrior, which also came in especially handy through that period. SueJean was present for the entire time that I was receiving and putting out the Revelation radio messages. I asked SueJean to write her observations of what she experienced during that time, for this book. Following is her unedited submission in answer to that request.

SUEJEAN'S OBSERVATIONS

If anyone had ever told me that someday I'd be involved in the process of bringing forth a book of revelation on The Book of Revelation, (or any other Scriptures, for that matter), I'm sure my first reaction would have been unbelief. I'm still not sure of the path that brought me to be a part of this extraordinary series of revelations that have evolved into this book. All I can say for sure is that HIS hand was evident throughout the steps HE had ordered before me.

The Book of Revelation is for many believers that one illusionary book of future events that many of us had long hoped would stay in the future, far in the future! I've often heard it said that we, the people of this generation, are the last generation. Many try to hold that reality away from themselves with the thought that previous generations have always had people saying that very same thing. Be it the ever-increasing darkness of the world around us or some cultural shift, it seems clear that more people are echoing this phrase more than ever before in history.

However, it has occurred, this phrase took on a whole new level of meaning at Passover in the Hebrew year of 6008, (Gregorian year–2008). At that time, revelations concerning the Book of Revelation were released and forced all of us at Tsiyon Ministries to undergo a profound paradigm shift that moved the Book of Revelation with its cataclysmic events from a vague future scenario into a roadmap for the events of today.

Frightening? Overwhelmingly so, at times. My role as transcriptionist and editor put me a couple of weeks or so behind every radio program. In some ways, the gap seemed a blessing as I was able to somewhat hold off the initial impact of each message as I watched formerly faithful listeners drop off to the left and the right as the message overwhelmed them and drove them away.

In other ways, the gap increased my ongoing anxiety to be thrust into the midst of revelation that by its very nature had to alter the course of my life. For that gap allowed the news events of the world to act as overwhelming and undeniable confirmation of all that YHWH had chosen to reveal at this specific point in time. The message would go out about the imminent collapse of the economy and two weeks later, news events would bear out the confirming evidence. This happened week after week during this message.

Focusing on my tasks allowed me to process and digest the revelation messages in small daily doses that HE walked me through day by day. There were days when it was all I could do to keep moving forward as I slowly made the shift in my own understanding that the Book of Revelation had inexorably moved from some vague future to our present day reality.

The real beauty of YHWH's plans came to me somewhere in the revelation of the white horse rider. Once I was able to accept and even embrace the understanding that "we **are** the final generation", YHWH was able to use the rest of the revelation message to show me personally that I have a role to play in HIS plans and purposes for these last days.

These roles are there for all those that willingly stand up, step forward and lay down their lives before HIM. That *revelation* allowed me to see for the first time how much we, as individuals mean to HIM. As HE sends forth this message seeking HIS remnant people, HIS glorious Presence can only be increasingly more and more evident with each day that passes.

By the end of the Revelation messages, I found myself moved from a position of dread and fear concerning end-time events to a place of peace and even rejoicing to know that YHWH is in control of all things and nothing will prevent HIS will from being done and that is "good news" or the gospel for HIS people, the remnant of Israel. We will not be walking through these end-time events alone. HE will be watching over each of us as HIS Word promises. HE said, "I will never leave, nor forsake you" and I'm willing to "bet" my life on that promise.

May your hearts be stirred by this, HIS message of hope and encouragement for the coming days!

SueJean

DAWN'S OBSERVATIONS

In the early portion of the 2008 calendar year, we at *On The Road To Tsiyon* were preparing to honor the shmita year (year of release), which would begin in the spring of 2008. As we began recording a program about the shmita year, we had a sense that YHWH had already prepared a very special new year to start in the weeks ahead. We had a deep sense that now was the time, more so than any other, to draw even nearer to HIM. Each time Eliyahu prayed about the shmita year and what YHWH would have us do, he consistently heard the same message: "It is the year of release." We had the sense "release" meant a convergence that wasn't going to occur in exactly the same way as most folks would expect it to progress. Before long the radio program about the shmita year reached its air date, the new Biblical year had arrived, and Passover/Pesach was upon us. Friends, including SueJean, having traveled all the way from Thailand, joined us in our home for that Passover meal and celebration. (*On The Road To Tsiyon*, program #118, Air Date 04/04/08)

The Holy Spirit/Rauch was present in our midst. It was truly an amazing time—both spiritually and as a family. I'll share more about the timing of the family aspect of this particular Passover in a moment, as it is an integral part of the story of what happened. During this Passover, there was music and joy, worship and fellowship filling our home! YHWH set this appointment—and we had shown up for it, open to hear what HE wanted to say and do with HIS time.

Each of us were spending time in personal reflection and prayer as Eliyahu talked about the significance and importance of what Messiah did for us on the very famous Passover meal evening, also commonly known as "the Lord's last supper." As we were quietly praying, each one individually, I began to have a vision of Messiah joining in Eliyahu's words. It was as if the Spiritual and the physical world meshed into one before my eyes in this spectacular convergence. As a result, I understood the word "supernatural" in a new way! Having a spiritual vision was not something new for me—yet none of the previous visions were like this one. It was a moment set-apart in my mind unlike any other previous to it. At the time it was very odd to me—yet oddly familiar too, because Messiah was in it. I felt HIS presence. I knew HE was blessing Eliyahu in a new way.

From my perspective, this is the exact moment YHWH opened up what affectionately thereafter became known in my own mind as "the brain dump" by which HE delivered this message to Eliyahu. What I mean to say is, from that moment on, over the course of the Biblical calendar year, I witnessed YHWH imparting to Eliyahu ben David HIS revelation on the Book of Revelation.

This outpouring came so rapidly that Eliyahu was often unable to sleep at all due to the need he felt to express the message in its entirety and to get it all faithfully recorded as it was given to him. Anyone who has ever received revelation knows this process is hard work—and I can testify that Eliyahu was not at all lazy! He occupied himself wholeheartedly going about his Father's business. He was working as a man who knew his life, and I dare say every one of the lives of YAH's own, depended on getting it all recorded and available to YAH's family.

Eliyahu's process didn't stop there—no! He painstakingly researched and consulted every avenue of study to confirm and test by the Scriptures every aspect of the revelation he had received, not wanting to introduce human errors. The process was of a man driven to get it right—because he understood so very much was at stake. I had the sense then that he understood the consequences perhaps even more so than any of us ever did or would. When he was sure he had it just right, he would emerge from his study letting me know I was needed to record the next program(s) in the Revelation Series for *On The Road To Tsiyon*. We often spent hours on end and even days on end painstakingly recording everything before the next "brain dump" of revelation occurred, sending us back into the process again.

Interlaced with this process was countless prayer sessions—individually and corporately. It was so clear Eliyahu was in the grip of a very private and intimate spiritual encounter which was the fruit of countless hours spent previously and concurrently in prayer, in fellowship with Messiah and the Father, and in Scripture study. The process itself set Eliyahu apart, as none of his closest friends or family members wanted to even interrupt his prayer time, thinking, or study process any more than absolutely necessary, seeing the intensity and integrity with which he was laboring for the Kingdom. As the process unfolded, many countless hours of prayer and further revelation also occurred—too many to enumerate here, but each as amazing as the one previous to it and as life-changing in my own understanding level as I'm sure it will be or has been to you, having encountered it for yourself.

During the process, YHWH told Eliyahu what was going to happen and often showed him things no one else had ever talked about. Yet, prayer and other occurrences confirmed each of these things. Not long after the confirmation stage, these events started happening in real time. Reading the news was like reading the Book of Revelation—only we all knew what shocking news report was going to be next, after this shocking report we were reading today.

YHWH also instructed to write it down in a book so "the runners" could run HIS message. In a labor of love, SueJean typed transcripts of every program in the Revelation Series to help towards achieving that end. Eliyahu began the process of condensing and editing the programs into something that started to resemble a manuscript. It became apparent from the process that "the book" was really a series of books—as no one book could adequately hold the entire message that was given to Eliyahu and still be bound into one volume. After writing, re-writing, and editing, volume one was ready. This occurred during Passover week of 2009—exactly one year after this process began. (Hab 2:2-3)

I feel blessed and privileged to have been a personal witness to these events and to have been able to contribute to them, in whatever way I could. We found ourselves wearing many different hats in order to achieve everything that needed to be completed. Truly the Book of Revelation does carry an amazing blessing for those who read it and keep it—just as the Scripture foretells.

Previously, I mentioned I would also relate a bit of information on the personal level about what was happening within our family at this same time. I don't share this portion of our story for any other reason than to glorify YHWH. Ministry partners have told me, knowing about our family experiences which occurred concurrently, form its own testimony of this revelation on the Book of Revelation coming from YHWH.

In mid-Feb. 2008, our family was reunited after being separated for nearly four months. The tragic event that caused that separation occurred in Oct. 2007 when our then 10 year old son climbed a tree, had a nasty fall, and seriously injured himself. The medical staff pointed out miracle after miracle during the course of events ranging from the moments immediately after the fall and continuing during the time of our son's hospitalization. He was hospitalized from Oct. thru Feb. and he returned home in a wheelchair, paralyzed from his chest level downward—and this occurred despite the fact the medical staff did not expect him to survive the initial injury at all.

With YHWH's grace, our family weathered the storm of enduring the hospitalization, the immediate loss of my work/income, all of the physical therapy sessions and long-distance travel for follow-up care, the extensive medical training and implementation of doing all kinds of new and unexpected things. We did this while producing a weekly radio program, keeping up with daily ministry correspondence as best we could, homeschooling, and doing all of the aspects needed to publish this book on the Book of Revelation. Ministry partners say the fact that as a family we were able to weather this storm and still produce fruit for the Kingdom, as well as it being fruit of this quality, which they say they are not able to receive anywhere else, in and of itself is the most awesome testimony to YHWH.

May the meditation of our hearts as we go about growing more in HIM each day and focusing our lives about doing HIS will cause HIS Remnant to find their way to do likewise as we labor to overcome this world. Messiah has gone before us and has shown us the way to do likewise. Messiah said, "I have spoken these things to you so that you might have peace in Me. In the world you shall have tribulation, but be of good cheer. I have overcome the world." (Joh 16:33 MKJV)

Dawn

THE AUTHOR'S FINAL REMARKS

You have just read the observations of others regarding the origin of the message you have begun to explore by reading this book. Now, it is time for me to give account for myself regarding this message.

Through Passover week of 2008, in the Spirit, I viewed/experienced the scene in Heaven I have described in this book. This continued to happen over a period of many nights, until after Pentecost of that same year. Each night I saw the heavenly events and each day what I saw was confirmed to me through the Word and the Spirit. I included much of what I saw in radio programs immediately, which I began broadcasting thereafter, in early 2008.

I believe my experience in the Spirit to have been much like Enoch and Yochanan also reported. However, while Yochanan saw the last days, then future from His time, what I saw was occurring in real time. That's because we are living in the last days now. Consequently, I am a living witness of heavenly realities that occurred in real time from Passover to Pentecost of 2008, and are ongoing since then. As a witness, I am reporting the news I have observed.

Here is the crux of my testimony:

In 1967 A.D. the *times of the Gentiles* ended and we entered the final generation.

In 1967 A.D. Messiah's judgment of the religious system, which claims to represent Him, began. That 40 year judgment concluded in the Biblical year which began in the spring of 2007, with His rejection of that religious system.

The Heavenly Judgment Court was convened at Passover of 2008, commencing Judgment Day.

Soon after Judgment Court preliminaries, the Lamb stood up and took the Scroll from the Father's right hand, thus beginning His judgment upon the world, according to the Father's plan.

That act of *the Lamb standing* began *the Lamb's Day of Power*, which will continue from Heaven until it is time for Him to make His visible Return to the Earth, at which time He will visibly and in Person consummate the last of the Scroll judgments.

At Pentecost season of 2008 in Heaven, Messiah removed the first four seals from the Scroll, in rapid succession, releasing the Four Horsemen of Revelation.

The Four Horsemen are currently let loose into the world to influence and shape the flow of events in the earth, to eventually fulfill their respective missions. This is going on right now. This is the point we are at in relation to the Book of Revelation at this writing.

No further seals are expected to be opened until after the Four Horsemen have sufficiently progressed in their respective missions. This will take a period of years.

Perhaps you have sensed that the whole atmosphere of the world, not to mention the spiritual atmosphere, changed dramatically in 2008. The news released by this book explains the reason for the change you have sensed.

No change is greater than the change that has occurred regarding the religious system. I was shown, as I have shared in this book, that YHWH is effectively done with the religious system and has now turned His favor toward the believing remnant of Israel.

Messiah is controlling events during this judgment period to re-gather that faithful remnant of the twelve tribes of scattered Israel. They will form the core of the Spiritual Temple which will be a beacon of His Glory through the darkest period of man's experience on earth, now just over the horizon.

Messiah is sifting all of mankind by these Scroll judgments, to separate out the wicked from the righteous. Overcomers from all nations who emerge victorious through this sifting process are to be joined to the Spiritual Temple. All the wicked will end up willingly deceived by the anti-messiah and will eventually share in his fate–the lake of fire. The Judgment Day process, over a period of years, will give all inhabitants of the earth every reasonable opportunity to repent and be saved from this crooked generation.

It is a shame that it takes troubles and disaster to turn the hearts of some fully toward God, but such are the hard hearts of fallen man. In truth, all of these punishing judgments are nothing more than a release of what men have already brought upon their own heads through their own selfish and wicked deeds.

Dear reader, I earnestly and sincerely pray that you, having received this witness, and having read all of the supporting documentation in this book, and in the Scriptures, will act upon it, will endure in it, and will be counted with the righteous unto the end and beyond, unto blessed eternity in the New Jerusalem.

May all of us together, along with the *four live things* and the 24 *Elders*, all of the *Heavenly Hosts,* all of *the righteous* of all ages, and all restored *Creation,* join together in the eternal chorus forever more: "All praise, honor and glory to the One seated on the Throne, and to the Lamb! They alone are worthy!" Amen and amen!

He is coming quickly and every eye will see Him–and He will see <u>them</u>, to give to each one according to each one's works.

In His Name and by His grace alone, I bear true witness as His servant and yours,

Eliyahu ben David

Conventions and Bibliography
Messianic Revelation Series: Volume 1
Announcing: Judgment Day

The first time you read this book you will probably want to read right through it as you would any book. However, after you have done that, you may want to study the content more deeply. I have included the information here to encourage use of this book in your Scripture studies.

SCRIPTURE USAGE AND CONVENTIONS HEREIN

Hebrew Names Version (HNV) of the *World English Bible* is a Modern English update of the acclaimed *American Standard Version* of 1901. Copyright is in the public domain. Unless otherwise noted Scripture verses herein are from the HNV, with some refinements noted as follows:

Spelling of the name *Yeshua* has been changed to *Y'shua* herein, to conform to the spelling of the Hebrew name that we otherwise use throughout this book. *The LORD* as used in the HNV is a substitute for the Divine Name, *YHWH*, in the original text. Therefore, we have restored YHWH to the text. Here, we leave it to the reader to choose the pronunciation of YHWH that he or she prefers, whether *Yahweh* or some other.

Capitalization of nouns and pronouns associated with divinity has been utilized herein. Names of all demonic entities are <u>not</u> capitalized in this work.

Other refinements have been made in specific verses that more accurately convey the meaning of the original text. Such changes are explained with appropriate references within the main text of this book.

"Old Testament" and "New Testament" are terms used universally in common reference works quoted in this book, forcing us to retain these terms to some extent. Therefore, to avoid confusion and for the sake of readability we have retained "OT" and "NT" as abbreviations representing the two library divisions of Scripture, respectively, that together comprise the recognized inspired canon of *All Scripture*. (2Ti 3:16)

Scripture references interlaced throughout this book have been provided for further study. To facilitate ease of use these references are found at the end of each related paragraph rather than in footnotes or endnotes. Abbreviations of Bible books used herein follow standard abbreviations as used in e-Sword Bible software. A chart of these Bible Book abbreviations follows.

Name	Abbrev
Genesis (B'Reyshith, Beginnings)	Gen
Exodus (Shemoth, The Words)	Exo
Leviticus (WaYiqra, And He Said)	Lev
Numbers (BaMidbar, In the Wilderness)	Num
Deuteronomy (Devarim, Rep. of the Covenant)	Deu
Joshua (Yehoshua)	Jos
Judges (Shoftim)	Jdg
Ruth	Rth
1 Samuel (1 Shmu'el)	1Sa
2 Samuel (2 Shmu'el)	2Sa
1 Kings (1 Melachim)	1Ki
2 Kings (2 Melachim)	2Ki
1 Chronicles (1 Dibri HaYamim)	1Ch
2 Chronicles (2 Dibri HaYamim)	2Ch
Ezra	Ezr
Nehemiah (Nechemyah)	Neh
Job (Iyov)	Job
Esther (Magillah of Hadassah)	Est
Psalms (Tehillim)	Psa
Proverbs (Mashley Shlomo)	Pro
Ecclesiastes (Qoheleth, The Preacher)	Ecc
Song of Solomon (Shir HaShirim)	Son
Isaiah (Yeshayahu)	Isa
Jeremiah (Yirmyahu)	Jer
Lamentations (Eychah)	Lam
Ezekiel (Yechezqel)	Eze
Daniel	Dan
Hosea	Hos
Joel (Yoel)	Joe
Amos	Amo
Obadiah (Ovadyah)	Oba
Jonah (Yonah)	Jon
Micah (Micha)	Mic
Nahum (Nachum)	Nah
Habbakuh (Havaqquq)	Hab
Zepaniah (Tsefanyah)	Zep
Haggai (Haggay)	Hag
Zechariah (Zecharyah)	Zec
Malachi	Mal

Name	Abbrev
Matthew (Mattithyahu)	Mat
Mark (Markos)	Mar
Luke (Lukas)	Luk
John (Yochanan)	Joh
Acts	Act
Romans	Rom
1 Corinthians	1Co
2 Corinthians	2Co
Galatians	Gal
Ephesians	Eph
Philippians	Phl
Colossians	Col
1 Thessalonians	1Th
2 Thessalonians	2Th
1 Timothy (1 Timotheos)	1Ti
2 Timothy (2 Timotheos)	2Ti
Titus (Titos)	Tit
Philemon (Filemon)	Phm
Hebrews (Messianic Jews)	Heb
James (Yaakov)	Jam
1 Peter (1 Kefa)	1Pe
2 Peter (2 Kefa)	2Pe
1 John (1 Yochanan)	1Jo
2 John (2 Yochanan)	2Jo
3 John (1 Yochanan)	3Jo
Jude (Yehudah)	Jud
Revelation	Rev

STRONG'S NUMBER USAGE AND CONVENTIONS HEREIN

Strong, James, *The New Strong's Complete Dictionary of Bible Words* (Nashville, 1996) Note: Many versions of this beloved standard abound.

Strong's Numbers are used in many reference works to help the reader easily find the English meanings of Hebrew and Greek words used in Scripture texts. James Strong assigned a unique number to every word of the Hebrew and Greek text of the Scriptures. Today, when you see those numbers cited, you can look up the meaning of the Hebrew or Greek word in Strong's Dictionary or in any of the countless other reference works that have adopted Strong's numbers. In this book Hebrew and Greek words are shown with the Strong's number to aid you in further study of the cited word.

BIBLE SOFTWARE REFERENCES USED

e-Sword: I do a lot of my basic study using free e-Sword software, and I highly recommend it. Frankly, I find it more comprehensive and user-friendly than the expensive Bible software I used in the past, before installing e-Sword several years ago. By including e-Sword here I hope to introduce this excellent free study resource to readers who may not have looked into it yet. A huge and growing number of Bibles, commentaries, dictionaries, graphics and Scripture study resources are available for use with e-Sword online at www.e-sword.net. Other resources for e-Sword are available from assorted web publishers. Many of these resources are classic standards, while some of the latest cutting-edge resources are also available for a small fee. I consulted many of the Bibles and reference works available in e-Sword in doing research for this book. By the way, utilizing Strong's numbering in your Scripture study is a snap using E-Sword!

PRINT BOOKS CITED OR CONSULTED HEREIN

benDavid, E., *Holy Order Restored*, (Zarach, 2007).

Bullinger, E.W., *The Apocalypse, or, The Day of the Lord* (Grand Rapids, 2nd edition 1909).

Charles, R. H., *The Book of Enoch* (London, 1917 edition).

Charlesworth, James, *The Old Testament Pseudepigrapha, Volume 1: Apocalyptic Literature and Testaments* (New Haven, 1983).

Collins, John, *The Apocalyptic Imagination: An Introduction to Jewish Apocalyptic Literature* (Grand Rapids, 1998).

Christianity Today, *Greek-English New Testament, Greek Text, Literal Interlinear, King James Version, New International Version* (Carol Stream, 1975).

Cross, F. L., *The Oxford Dictionary of the Christian Church* (Oxford, 1958).

Cyrus Gordon and Gary Rendsburg, *The Bible And The Ancient Near East,* (New York, 1997).

Funk and Wagnalls, *Jewish Encyclopedia* (New York, 1901).

Godet, F.L., *Studies on the New Testament* (San Francisco, 1984).

Gregg, Steve, *Revelation: Four Views: A Parallel Commentary* (Nashville, 1997).

Harrison, E.F., *Introduction to the New Testament*, (Grand Rapids, Revised 1971).

LaHaye , Tim, *Revelation Unveiled, (*Grand Rapids, 1999).

Laurence, Richard, *The Book of Enoch* (London, 1883).

Lumpkin, Joseph B., *The Lost Book of Enoch: A Comprehensive Transliteration of The Forgotten Book of The Bible* (Blountsville, 2004).

Schoettgen, Christian, *Horoe Hebraicoe et Talmudicoe* (Dresden, 1733).

Thayer, Joseph H., *Thayer's Greek-English Lexicon of the New Testament* (Peabody, 1996).

W.E. Vine, Merrill F. Unger, William White Jr., *Vine's Complete Expository Dictionary of Old and New Testament Words* (Nashville, 1996).

TEN WORDS OF THE TESTIMONY

1. "I am YHWH your God, Who brought you out of the land of Egypt, out of the house of bondage. You shall have no other gods before Me."

2. "You shall not make for yourselves an idol, nor any image of anything that is in the heavens above, or that is in the earth beneath, or that is in the water under the earth: you shall not bow yourself down to them, nor serve them, for I, YHWH your God, am a jealous God, visiting the iniquity of the fathers on the children, on the third and on the fourth generation of those who hate Me, and showing loving kindness to thousands of those who love Me and keep My commandments."

3. "You shall not take the Name of YHWH your God in vain, for YHWH will not hold him guiltless who takes His Name in vain."

4. "Remember the Sabbath day, to keep it holy. You shall labor six days, and do all your work, but the seventh day is a Sabbath to YHWH your God. You shall not do any work in it, you, nor your son, nor your daughter, your male servant, nor your female servant, nor your livestock, nor your stranger who is within your gates; for in six days YHWH made heaven and earth, the sea, and all that is in them, and rested the seventh day; therefore YHWH blessed the Sabbath day, and made it holy."

5. "Honor your father and your mother, that your days may be long in the land which YHWH your God gives you."

6. "You shall not murder."

7. "You shall not commit adultery."

8. "You shall not steal."

9. "You shall not give false testimony against your neighbor."

10. "You shall not covet your neighbor's house. You shall not covet your neighbor's wife, nor his male servant, nor his female servant, nor his ox, nor his donkey, nor anything that is your neighbor's."

𐤅𐤉𐤃𐤁𐤓 𐤀𐤋𐤄𐤉 𐤀𐤕 𐤊𐤋 𐤄𐤃𐤁𐤓𐤉 𐤄𐤀𐤋𐤄
𐤋𐤀𐤌𐤓 𐤀𐤍𐤊𐤉 𐤉𐤄𐤅𐤄 𐤀𐤋𐤄𐤉 𐤀𐤔𐤓
𐤄𐤅𐤑𐤀𐤕𐤉 𐤌𐤀𐤓 𐤌𐤑𐤓𐤉 𐤌𐤁𐤉𐤕 𐤏𐤁𐤃𐤉𐤌
𐤋𐤀 𐤉𐤄𐤉𐤄 𐤋 𐤀𐤋𐤄𐤉 𐤀𐤇𐤓𐤉 𐤏𐤋 𐤐𐤍𐤉

𐤋𐤀 𐤕𐤏𐤔𐤄 𐤋 𐤐𐤎𐤋 𐤅𐤊𐤋 𐤕𐤌𐤅𐤍𐤄 𐤀𐤔𐤓
𐤁𐤔𐤌𐤉 𐤌𐤌𐤏𐤋 𐤅𐤀𐤔𐤓 𐤁𐤀𐤓 𐤌𐤕𐤇𐤕 𐤅𐤀𐤔𐤓
𐤁𐤌𐤉 𐤌𐤕𐤇𐤕 𐤋𐤀𐤓𐤑

𐤋𐤀 𐤕𐤔𐤕𐤇𐤅𐤄 𐤋𐤄 𐤅𐤋𐤀 𐤕𐤏𐤁𐤃 𐤊𐤉 𐤀𐤍𐤊𐤉
𐤉𐤄𐤅𐤄 𐤀𐤋𐤄𐤉 𐤀𐤋 𐤒𐤍𐤀 𐤐𐤒𐤃 𐤏𐤅 𐤀𐤁𐤕
𐤏𐤋 𐤁𐤍𐤉 𐤏𐤋 𐤔𐤋𐤔𐤉 𐤅𐤏𐤋 𐤓𐤁𐤏𐤉 𐤋𐤔𐤍𐤀𐤉
𐤅𐤏𐤔𐤄 𐤇𐤎𐤃 𐤋𐤀𐤋𐤐𐤉 𐤋𐤀𐤄𐤁𐤉 𐤅𐤋𐤔𐤌𐤓𐤉
𐤌𐤑𐤅𐤕𐤉

𐤋𐤀 𐤕𐤔𐤀 𐤀𐤕 𐤔 𐤉𐤄𐤅𐤄 𐤀𐤋𐤄𐤉 𐤋𐤔𐤅𐤀
𐤊𐤉 𐤋𐤀 𐤉𐤍𐤒𐤄 𐤉𐤄𐤅𐤄 𐤀𐤕 𐤀𐤔𐤓 𐤉𐤔𐤀 𐤀𐤕
𐤔𐤌𐤅 𐤋𐤔𐤅𐤀

𐤆𐤊𐤅𐤓 𐤀𐤕 𐤉𐤅 𐤄𐤔𐤁𐤕 𐤋𐤒𐤃𐤔𐤅
𐤔𐤔𐤕 𐤉𐤌𐤉 𐤕𐤏𐤁𐤃 𐤅𐤏𐤔𐤉𐤕 𐤊𐤋 𐤌𐤋𐤀𐤊𐤕𐤊
𐤅𐤉𐤅 𐤄𐤔𐤁𐤉𐤏𐤉 𐤔𐤁𐤕 𐤋𐤉𐤄𐤅𐤄 𐤀𐤋𐤄𐤉
𐤋𐤀 𐤕𐤏𐤔𐤄 𐤊𐤋 𐤌𐤋𐤀𐤊𐤄 𐤀𐤕𐤄 𐤅𐤁𐤍 𐤅𐤁𐤕𐤊
𐤏𐤁𐤃 𐤅𐤀𐤌𐤕 𐤅𐤁𐤄𐤌𐤕 𐤅𐤂𐤓 𐤀𐤔𐤓
𐤁𐤔𐤏𐤓𐤉 𐤊𐤉 𐤔𐤔𐤕 𐤉𐤌𐤉 𐤏𐤔𐤄 𐤉𐤄𐤅𐤄
𐤀𐤕 𐤄𐤔𐤌𐤉 𐤅𐤀𐤕 𐤄𐤀𐤓 𐤀𐤕 𐤄𐤉 𐤅𐤀𐤕
𐤊𐤋 𐤀𐤔𐤓 𐤁 𐤅𐤉𐤍𐤇 𐤁𐤉𐤅 𐤄𐤔𐤁𐤉𐤏𐤉
𐤏𐤋 𐤊 𐤁𐤓 𐤉𐤄𐤅𐤄 𐤀𐤕𐤉𐤅 𐤄𐤔𐤁𐤕 𐤅𐤉𐤒𐤃𐤔𐤄𐤅

𐤊𐤁𐤃 𐤀𐤕 𐤀𐤁𐤉 𐤅𐤀𐤕 𐤀𐤌 𐤋𐤌𐤏 𐤉𐤀𐤓𐤊𐤅𐤍
𐤉𐤌𐤉 𐤏𐤋 𐤄𐤀𐤃𐤌𐤄 𐤀𐤔𐤓 𐤉𐤄𐤅𐤄 𐤀𐤋𐤄𐤉𐤊
𐤍𐤕 𐤋𐤊

𐤋𐤀 𐤕𐤓𐤑𐤇

𐤋𐤀 𐤕𐤍𐤀𐤐

𐤋𐤀 𐤕𐤂𐤍𐤁

𐤋𐤀 𐤕𐤏𐤍𐤄 𐤁𐤓𐤏 𐤏𐤃 𐤔𐤒𐤓
𐤋𐤀 𐤕𐤇𐤌𐤃 𐤁𐤉𐤕 𐤓𐤏 𐤋𐤀 𐤕𐤇𐤌𐤃 𐤀𐤔𐤕
𐤓𐤏 𐤅𐤏𐤁𐤃𐤅 𐤅𐤀𐤌𐤕𐤅 𐤅𐤔𐤅𐤓𐤅 𐤅𐤇𐤌𐤓𐤅 𐤅𐤊𐤋
𐤀𐤔𐤓 𐤋𐤓𐤏𐤊

Revelation Series Audio CD Order Form

Wish you hadn't missed the original *On The Road To Tsiyon* programs? Want to hear Eliyahu ben David sharing this Revelation message in his own words? Now you can! Order all 29 programs in the Revelation Unsealed Series on audio CDs below. CDs below are offered free with a contribution of $6.00 US each to cover shipping and handling. Check off the ones you want, fill in your information on the other side, and send this order form in to the address on the other side.

Check off the CDs you want ($6.00 US per CD)

Rev Foundations-6 CDs

- ☐ Rev Foundations #122
- ☐ Rev Judgment-House of God #123
- ☐ Rev Judgment-Churches #124
- ☐ Enter the Throneroom #125
- ☐ The King's Response #126
- ☐ Worthy is the Lamb! #127

4 Horsemen of Rev-Pt 1-5 CDs

- ☐ 4 Horsemen Of Rev Overview #128
- ☐ White Horse Rider Fallacies #129
- ☐ The White Horse Rider #130
- ☐ More White Horse Rider #131
- ☐ Red Horse Rider-Envtl War #132

4 Horsemen of Rev-Pt 2-5 CDs

- ☐ Black Horse Rider 1 #133
- ☐ Black Horse Rider 2 #134
- ☐ Black Horse Rider 3 #135
- ☐ Pale Horse-Catastrophe #136
- ☐ Pale Horse Rider Scenarios #137

Unto The Tribulation-6 CDs

- ☐ 5th Seal How Long O Lord? #138
- ☐ 5th Seal Scenario #139
- ☐ 6th Seal Signs in the Sky #140
- ☐ 6th Seal Heavens Like a Scroll #141
- ☐ 7th-Tribulation Commencement #142
- ☐ 6th &7th Seal Defeat of Gog #143

144000 Unto The Kingdom-7 CDs

- ☐ Sunrise Messenger-144000 #144
- ☐ Numbering The 144000 #145
- ☐ 144000 & the Great Multitude #146
- ☐ 144000 Stand On Mt Tsiyon #147
- ☐ Now Is Come The Kingdom #148
- ☐ Rev Relevancy #149
- ☐ Rev What Now? #150

More great Tsiyon radio programs are available at:

www.Tsiyon.org

☐ **I want all the CDs! I will also receive a Bonus copy of the Tsiyon Bound interview. I'm sending $174 US**

Please Print Your Address Info On Other Side

Special CD Offer for Book Readers:

Shalom! Eliyahu here. Thank you for reading my book. I'm offering book readers a special opportunity to obtain audio CDs of the radio programs that inspired this Messianic Revelation Series book series. Check off the CDs you want on the other side of this order form, fill out the form below, and mail it to the "Send To" address listed below.

Fill in the form below for this special offer.
Please print legibly.

Name: ______________________________

Street: ______________________________

Other: ____________________ Total # of CDs: (from other side) __________ X $6.00 ea.

City: ____________________

State: ____________________ Total CD Donation: __________

Country: ____________________ Any Ministry Donation: __________

Code: ____________________ Total Remitted: __________

Send To:

Tsiyon (Make checks to "Tsiyon")
1511 S. Texas Ave #297
College Station, TX, USA 77840

May you be blessed in your study of HIS Word!